After breaking her back in a car accident in 2008, **Nikki Emerson** was determined her paralysis and her wheelchair would make no difference to the way she lived her life. This turned out not to be the case though. Instead, they had a positive impact, exposing her to a wealth of incredible things she would never have dreamed of had she not become disabled.

Nikki Emerson

Nikki Emerson

Constable • London

Constable & Robinson Ltd
55–56 Russell Square
London WC1B 4HP
www.constablerobinson.com

First published in the UK by Constable,
an imprint of Constable & Robinson Ltd, 2014

A copy of the British Library Cataloguing in
Publication Data is available from the British Library.

ISBN: 978-1-78033-865-1 (paperback)

Typeset by TW Typesetting, Plymouth, Devon

Printed and bound in the UK by CPI Group (UK) Ltd

1 3 5 7 9 10 8 6 4 2

For my incredible family

Prologue

I'm told it's a pretty harrowing experience when the doctors inform you for the first time that you're not going to walk again. To be honest I was so drugged up after the spinal surgery to set my broken back that my main recollection is of the slightly batty woman in the bed opposite shouting 'Lucifer!' at the nurses on the other side of the very ineffectual screen my consultant had constructed to give us some privacy. He could have told me I would dance for the Royal Ballet in two weeks – I doubt if my reaction would have been very different. On 30 June 2008 at around 2.30 p.m. my car skidded across two lanes and spun off the Oxford ring road, flipping over on the verge and hitting a tree down the bank. The tree then fell on the car, pushing the sliding seat I was in into the steering wheel, with me in the middle. A bit of a comedy of errors really, but I was lucky in that I escaped with only three broken bones and a punctured lung – from the outside I looked totally unscathed. Unfortunately, though, one of the broken bones was my T10 vertebra, the point of the spine just below my ribcage, and as a result I'm totally paralysed from the hips down. Ironically, I was studying neuroscience at Oxford University when I crashed so I knew exactly what I'd done to myself. They don't tell you how much it hurts in the textbooks though!

Fast-forward then through my morphine days at the John Radcliffe Hospital, where I'm told I made very little sense although I remember with absolute clarity the Wimbledon men's singles final being played with a canary in the place of the tennis ball, to an intense ten weeks of rehabilitation (or in my opinion a fun summer camp on wheels). From the moment I was transferred to Stoke Mandeville National Spinal Injuries Centre (NSIC) in Buckinghamshire I was fixated on getting to physiotherapy so I could learn how to fix my legs. You can imagine my disappointment when my lovely physiotherapist Selina explained that she wouldn't be able to make me walk; her job was to teach me how to get around without my legs. That's when it hit home that this wasn't something I could just fix and move on from.

Of course I didn't totally give up hope. I'm extremely stubborn and from the moment I broke my back, and everyone started coming in with bad news and sympathy, my brain started an infuriating game of 'glass half full' totally of its own accord. As much as I wanted to scream and cry for days I couldn't seem to stop finding the positive side of the situation, which I guess in the end is what so quickly got me out of rehab and back into doing sport as I always had before I broke my back. People keep telling me I was 'so strong' after my accident but that's just not true. My parents and my friends were strong. I didn't even try to deal with the emotional side of what had happened; I just picked out the good bits and moved on to the next challenge.

The hardest thing to get used to was people's reactions when they came to visit and saw me in my wheelchair. When I was lying in a hospital bed nobody showed any awkwardness – I was just a sick person who would get better. The wheelchair made it all a bit real and a lot of people didn't come back after seeing me pushing around in it. I lost a lot of friends in those ten weeks. Many of them returned as my race results picked up and they saw interviews I'd done or photos on Facebook showing that I'm still the same as I ever was – I just sit down a lot more. Or perhaps they finally realized that spinal cord injury isn't actually contagious. The friends who stayed when I was in hospital and the new ones I've made since then are the only ones I have any time for though (even if they do steal my chair for races the second I'm out of it and see my lap as the nearest vacant seat!).

My first experience of Paralympic sport came while still in rehab at the NSIC. During my stay there I tried many wheelchair sports, from tennis to hockey to basketball, and although I enjoyed them I saw them as inferior adaptations of their Olympic counterparts. That changed when the Beijing Paralympics started. I'd never paid much attention to the Paralympics – in fact I'm not even sure I knew they were taking place after the Olympics in 2008 – but being in hospital adapting to life in a wheelchair seemed like a pretty good time to start taking an interest.

The event that sticks in my mind from the Beijing coverage is the T54 women's 5000 m final. In wheelchair racing there are six classes, including two for people with brain injuries. The T54 class is for the least disabled wheelchair athletes, the majority of whom have low spinal lesions or amputations to their lower limbs, although in the 5000 m the T53 and T54 athletes race together under the T54 category. The only people in wheelchairs I'd been exposed to at that point were my fellow spinal injury patients and a few of the mentors who visited the hospital, and I'd pretty much accepted that I'd never get back to my former athletic build and would always carry the label 'disabled person' or worse, 'wheelchair bound'. Then the camera panned along the start line showing women who looked as strong and lean as the athletes in the Olympic Games and whose disability, although highlighted by the fact they raced in wheelchairs, would never be at the front of any-one's mind. When the race started, the speed at which the girls went both surprised me and held massive appeal. As a big cycling fan I was interested to see a pack develop just like the peloton in the Tour de France, and by the time a crash occurred, taking out the front of the field, I was hooked. Paralympic sport all of a sudden didn't seem inferior. In fact I'd be surprised if anyone could find an able-bodied women's 5000 m race better viewing than its wheelchair equivalent.

Fast-forward a few years and I was competing against those girls I saw on TV racing in Beijing. I still got a bit starstruck now and then when I lined up beside the people who inspired me to get into Paralympic sport, but after two years on the athletics circuit I got to know them and even beat some of them. It was a steep learning curve, trying to get by in a sport I didn't understand among people who had been racing for years before I'd even heard of wheelchair racing, but thanks to my brilliant first coach Ian Thompson and his wife Tanni's no-holds-barred approach I gradually moved up from regularly finishing last in the slowest heat at domestic track meets to not disgracing myself in the finals at international meets. I knocked exactly an hour off my London Marathon time between 2009 and 2010, which shows just how good a coach Ian is. I used to complain about being out in the snow unable to feel my hands and taking my gloves off at the end of the session to find them blistered and bloody, but there's no question that it gets results!

I started racing as a bit of a joke really. Ian suggested I come to the Silverstone Half Marathon, one week after my first (and only) training session, to watch but I ended up taking part and achieved the qualifying time for the 2009 London Wheelchair Marathon. Six weeks later I completed the marathon and by the time I crossed the finish line I was hooked. There's nothing like the feeling of freewheeling down Shooters Hill with thousands of people cheering on either side to get an adrenaline junkie like me addicted. As my first international race the London Marathon was a bit of a baptism of fire as it's one of the few televised wheelchair races in the UK and one of the even fewer with decent prize money, so it attracts a lot of international athletes. For any professional athlete, Olympic or Paralympic, winning is the number-one goal, and medalling at a big event like London can fund the rest of the season for a top Paralympic athlete.

Fast-forward five years and I'll be watching the 2014 London Marathon from the Help for Heroes cheering station where the company I work for volunteer. In the short time since I broke my back my life has been a crazy mix of ups, downs, but most importantly incredible opportunities. This book gives an insight into the exciting and often hilarious world of disability athletics through my experiences, and into my version of 'real life' after giving up racing. I hope that by the end you'll come to realize just as I have that being disabled has no more bearing on someone's ability to achieve any goal than their gender or skin colour. What's important is to work hard, be willing to give anything a try, and never let anyone else decide what you can and can't do on your behalf.

1

The Accident

I'm not sure whether being able to remember the car crash that broke my back is a blessing or a curse. On the positive side, the fact that I stayed conscious probably saved my life. But during the many nights I woke up in Stoke Mandeville NSIC in total panic, thinking that I was once again trapped upside down in my car on the A40, I definitely resented having those memories! Of course after a few moments the familiar country scene on the hospital curtains would come into focus and I'd feel the stickiness of the plastic mattress under my back and realize that my immobility was not due to my car seat wedging me against the steering wheel, but a result of my torso and legs being paralysed from the bottom of my ribs down.

On 30 June 2008 I had just returned from a weekend by the pool at my oldest school friend's house near Hastings via Oxford, where I had just finished my second year studying neuroscience and psychology. It was a beautifully sunny weekend and having finished my second year finals I was free to relax and enjoy catching up with old friends. After a birthday lunch with another school friend, I left the city to visit my then boyfriend who lived in Birmingham, and a few minutes into the drive my car skidded on the ring road and I lost control of it, spinning first into the gravel on the edge of the outside lane and then sliding across the lanes and down the grassy bank of the central reservation, where the car flipped over. Surprisingly I didn't feel scared at all during this real-life rollercoaster; I kept hearing my dad saying 'steer into the skid' as he had years before when teaching me to drive on frosty winter mornings. Unfortunately it seems that that tip only works on ice though!

So there I was, upside down among the trees, my little red Peugeot 106 invisible from the road and the front of my car concertinaed by the tree that broke its skidding path over the grass. Then the tree fell on the car and I felt an intense pain at the back of my head, like I'd been kicked by someone wearing toe-capped boots. I tried to squeeze out from behind the steering wheel but the sliding seat had broken free during the impact and slid forward before locking itself back into place up against the steering wheel. The gap was too narrow to escape without first pushing the seat back, and my legs were not responding to my brain's pleas to push. To be honest I saw no reason to panic as I assumed my spinal cord had just gone into shock from the blow. I didn't give any consideration to the prospect of this inactivity in my lower body being permanent – after all, things like that don't happen to you, do they?

My main priority then became getting air into my lungs, taking deep breaths while trying to block out the sound of Edith Bowman presenting Glastonbury Festival on Radio 1 as I thought through my options. I've always been a logical and positive person and I needed those traits in a big way to get through those claustrophobic hours. Unfortunately the deep breaths were slightly impeded by the sensation of having an iron corset around my ribs brought about by neuropathic pain due to the injury to my spinal cord, and by the rib piercing my left lung and rendering it pretty useless as a gas-exchange device. At that point, I did begin to panic! It felt like I sat for hours focusing on trying to take in enough air to stay conscious and shout for help, and groping for the sliding-seat mechanism to try to remove some of the compression on my ribcage. In reality though it can't have been more than a few minutes before a pair of upside-down boat shoes appeared at my window. The owner of the shoes didn't say anything and I never saw his face but I'm eternally grateful to him for calling the fire crew who arrived to painstakingly cut me out of the wreckage over the next three hours.

It's pretty amazing the capacity the human body has to deal with trauma – and indeed the human mind's capacity to deal with the same also astounds me. As soon as the firefighters had cut a large enough hole in the car door for one of them to reach through with a mask to hover over my face, it was as though my lungs could finally admit defeat. They gave in to the assistance offered to them by the tanks of oxygen pumping through the tubes and erratically getting into my nose and mouth as I struggled to hold my head close enough to the mask to get any benefit. Breathing became more and more difficult as the pain down my spine and around my chest grew and my adrenaline levels began to fall. I drifted in and out of lucidity, repeating over and over in my head 'stay awake, stay awake' as the firefighters continued to urge me to do. They asked me inane questions to keep me conscious and I babbled in response, repeatedly calling them 'sir' as I couldn't focus enough to remember their names. I remember begging one fireman who was holding the oxygen mask over my face to give me a pair of scissors to cut my belt off as I thought that was what was compressing my ribs. In hindsight I wish I hadn't done that – it was a really great belt and its removal didn't help my breathing situation at all!

I'd love to say I heard voices calling to me through a bright haze or saw my life flash before my eyes as I teetered on the brink of consciousness, but actually I just heard the voice of the fireman holding my oxygen mask mingled with the continued babble of Radio 1 and saw lots of foliage below me and my burning yet useless legs above me. Needless to say my back hurt like hell, but the burning in my legs as a result of the spinal nerve damage was much, much worse. Thankfully I barely notice it anymore but at that time had someone told me I'd have pins and needles in my legs for the rest of my life I probably would have asked them to shoot me!

Eventually the crew managed to right the car and get me out. I've no doubt that the unresponsiveness of my legs helped to speed up this process, as it made it pretty obvious that my spinal cord was already damaged, so the priority was to get me out of the car rather than needing to protect my back too much. I don't remember much about the ambulance ride to the John Radcliffe Hospital in Oxford, but I do remember begging not to be taken there due to my inexplicable fear of hospitals. I think the paramedics thought I was rambling deliriously, but I was totally serious about wanting to avoid going inside a hospital at all costs! Once I was admitted to A&E I'm pretty sure I blacked out with the pain of being poked and prodded and having what felt like hundreds of tubes inserted into my bruised and battered body. It was a baptism of fire into what was to come during my subsequent time in the John Radcliffe and Stoke Mandeville – it's true what they say about your body not belonging to you anymore once you've been given a hospital bracelet. I felt like a pincushion by the time they released me in a borrowed wheelchair to face the world from my new and rather diminutive height eleven weeks later!

2

John Radcliffe Hospital Trauma Ward

It felt as though I was watching the initial blur of doctors and nurses cutting off my white vest top and shorts and attacking me with tubes and needles during my admission to A&E rather than taking any part in it. I dimly remember the ceiling being grey with a metal pipe running above my head but the rest of the room was a haze of pain. While I was being cut out of my car by the firemen, I was able to talk and although I was in pain I didn't feel like I was in a critical state. It seems as though the emergency doctors didn't agree though as they informed the police that I might not make it through the night. Knowing that now, I've tried to think back and remember what it felt like to be 'dying' in medical terms but, if I'm honest, aside from the pain in my back and around my ribs I've felt worse when I had a bad bout of flu. Breathing was difficult as I'd punctured a lung but with the help of oxygen tubes into my nose, which I hated and pulled out so that the oxygen came out just under my nostrils and had the same effect without tubes scratching at me, I could still breathe. I had a blood transfusion to counteract the internal bleeding, and once I'd been moved onto an uncomfortable plastic hospital bed and surrounded by crunchy white pillows it was quite nice to get some rest after a busy weekend.

A few minutes after I had arrived in the trauma ward and was lying in bed, a male and a female police officer came to see me. They asked if I'd been drink-driving. I felt like they thought I'd committed a criminal act rather than had an unlucky accident. Simultaneously a different set of police had arrived at my parents' house, blue lights wailing. Mum was up at the stables beside their home looking after her horses and walked down the path to the house when she saw the police car. It didn't occur to her that there was anything to worry about. Even when the police officer told her she needed to get to the John Radcliffe Hospital quickly as I'd been in a bad car crash it still didn't sink in and she assumed I'd broken an ankle, at worst, and would recover quickly. The police officer kept asking her if she understood as she was so calm and in no hurry to get into the car with him. She even insisted on going to change her clothes before setting off for the hospital! It was only when she was finally on her way to Oxford in the police car and the officer turned on the flashing lights that it dawned on her that perhaps the accident had been more serious than she'd assumed.

Once that initial blur of doctors stabilizing me and police

interrogating me came to a close the first thing on my mind was that my friend Rachel and my then boyfriend would be worried about why I hadn't arrived in Birmingham and I had to get a message to them. Looking back I really should have been more concerned that my family should know I was in hospital but that didn't really occur to me. Unfortunately the only phone number I could remember was that of my friend Ceci, who was in Italy at the time and must have been slightly shocked to receive a phone call from a nurse asking for Rachel's number as I was in hospital! Ceci was brilliant in passing on the news to my closest friends, in particular to Lou, who immediately tagged all my friends in a Facebook note so they all knew what had happened and where I was for visiting. She kept this note updated after every one of her daily visits to me and fielded all the well-wishing messages that I wasn't yet strong enough either mentally or physically to respond to for the first few weeks after my injury. All of my friends were fantastic during the eleven weeks I spent in hospital but Lou in particular has probably kept a ward afloat with the cash she spent on hospital parking. The nurses at Stoke joked that she should move in there as she was around so much!

By the time all that had been worked out Mum had arrived in a pretty panicked state and was fairly unimpressed to find me still covered in blood, grit and bits of tree and begging anyone who would listen for some water. As usual it didn't take her long to sort everything and everyone out! I hadn't been given a drink as the nurses didn't

8

know how I'd drink it without being able to sit up. She found a straw. I hadn't had the blood and dirt washed off my face because they were worried about dislodging the tubes going into my nose. She washed around them. That pretty much sums up my mother's approach to everything – there's a solution to every problem if you look for it rather than worrying about it. As my time in hospital wore on it was a trait I came to appreciate more and more from her. I'd like to think I've inherited at least some of her problem-solving ability (and her inability to accept people saying no!) and that's what helped me to get through rehab so quickly.

Unfortunately my accident was poorly timed as NHS staff were working to rule so there were no surgeons willing to operate on my spine out of hours. The A&E department rang every university hospital from when I arrived there at 6 p.m. and were willing to airlift me any-where in the country but nobody was available. We even contacted a friend's father, who is an osteopathic surgeon, but by the time he'd have made it to Oxford we thought the resident surgeons would have come in for their morn-ing surgeries and I'd be operated on by one of them. How wrong we were. There's an eight-hour window in which your spinal cord can survive without oxygen and there's a chance that the nerves will come out of the spinal shock caused by being compressed if the pressure is relieved within this time. My spinal nerves weren't damaged by the break in my back so getting the pressure off them within this window was a critical determining factor in whether I would walk again. We waited and waited and eventually around 2 p.m. I went down to theatre – a full twenty-four hours after my accident. I was in theatre for five and a half hours, during which time the firemen who rescued me from the car came to visit. I was very sad not to get to see them as they really did save my life and I'd love to have been able to thank them in person, though I did write a letter to them later.

I don't remember going down to surgery or being put under anaesthetic except vaguely having to sign a consent form in case I died. I do remember vividly coming to after my surgery, though, in a room full of beds with white curtains around my area and bright white lights. I felt tired and in pain, but thankfully one of the only parts of my body that didn't hurt was my head. A headache after spinal surgery is a strong indicator that the spinal cord has been damaged and spinal fluid has leaked out, and as my scans had shown that before surgery my spinal cord was intact I was very keen to keep it that way. My surgeon, who was actually a knee specialist which goes some way to explaining why the scar on my back is so neat, had put rods from the T12 vertebra up to the T6 vertebra to hold my spine together and had removed all the pieces of my T10 vertebra that were floating around in my back. I had eight screws holding the rods in place, one of which became loose a few weeks later during my rehab and is now pointlessly sitting in my back not holding anything much together. The recovery nurse was very nice and gave me water and chatted to me until they were happy that my vitals had stabilized. I didn't want to have to leave and go back to the crazy people on the trauma ward!

Abruptly I'm woken up by shouts of 'Lucifer! Lucifer!' The batty woman the other side of my ward has obviously been woken by the lovely black nurse who works the trauma ward shifts. Unfortunately crazy woman seems to be incurably racist.

A little while later I wake up again. I must have dozed off but now the night-time dose of morphine has worn off and my back is screaming in agony. It feels as though a thousand hot pokers are being driven into my spine and a straitjacket is constricting my breathing. I'm not sure if it was this that woke me again or the guy in the room across the hall who has been systematically throwing everything off his bedside table and is now shaking the rails of his bed to get the nurses' attention. I don't blame him as they seem to forget to give him water every day so eventually he gets desperate. Mum's been taking him drinks a few times a day so I'm not sure what he'll do when I leave – which will hopefully be soon.

It's the day after the operation to set my spine, two days after the car accident that brought me into hospital. I'm the first on the list to be seen so thankfully it's not long before my consultant arrives and puts screens up around my bed. I sort of register this is different to previous visits he's made to my bed but as at the moment they're still refusing to give me an IV morphine drip with an activator button to allow me to control my morphine dosages I'm not too focused on anything other than the pain of existing. He talks for a while and at some point 'you're not going to walk again' makes it through the haze surrounding my brain. Mum seems upset by this. I probably should be, too. Oh yeah, I think

11

I'm crying. Weird – it's like watching someone else being upset. The crying seems to have worked though, or maybe Mum has just thrown a big strop about me being on the crazy ward, because I'm being moved into a private room – awesome!

It's not a bad morning considering the news I've just received. My best friend Lou, whom I'd just dropped home before I crashed, is visiting as usual and I manage to keep down a cup of tea. I'm not up to doing much as the pain in my back is refusing to subside so we flick through Vogue *and chat a bit about how I'm going to get walking again. But then a few minutes later it all goes downhill very fast. The doctor has arrived! He pincushions me a couple of times before my veins decide to let him take blood. At least that pain's a distraction from my back. Oh wow, he's putting in a cannula. Could it finally be . . . ? Yes, an IV morphine drip. This stuff is going to be my friend. Click. Ooh, woozy feeling. But damn, still the same pain. Click again. More woozy. Oh cool, my legs are moving. Why does my back hurt? Did I fall over or something?*

Later that afternoon, still in my morphine haze, I register that my friend Arthur and my boyfriend have joined Lou by my bed. Ooh, the men's singles final at Wimbledon is on. Why am I in bed? And why are they hitting a canary over the net – is that something new for 2008? I don't like this. I think I'll close my eyes and have a sleep.

Oh no, Lou left her DVDs. I'll have to run them over to her before she gets out of the hospital. That's good, she hasn't got far. I catch her before she's even down the corridor. She'd have been gutted if I stole her Tudors *box set. But why is our friend Rob holding all her DVDs? He must have taken them back from her on his way in. Oh, that's annoying! I try to explain to him that I gave them back to her and I didn't run down the hall for nothing but he just looks upset. Men. Now he's trying to tell me I didn't chase her and that I can't run. OK, I might have lost shape during second-year exams but I can still run a few hundred metres.*

Waking up from naps is always the worst. Wow, my back hurts. And my ribs. I can't breathe. Why did Mum bother waking me up to eat that green gunge? That's not soup, it's toxic waste. Besides, my torso's so swollen I look pregnant, so eating is not high on my priority list! Click. But it's OK . . . maybe another nap.

Those first nights in hospital weren't ones I'd care to repeat. It was my first time in a hospital bed and I hated the way the sheets stuck to my already insanely painful body thanks to the horrible plastic mattress, and how I wasn't allowed to sit up at all so all my weight was on the break in my spine twenty-four hours a day. I was under constant observation with electrodes attached to my toe and stuck to my chest and a cannula in my arm. Everyone on the ward was a trauma patient so there was a constant cacophony of bleeps and alarms going off when blood-oxygen levels or pulse rates dropped, making it feel pretty spooky at night when all the lights went out. Mum stayed beside my bed all night and chatted to me quietly until the nurses came in at the crack of dawn to take my blood pressure and pulse rate with their familiar little trolley. My week at the John Radcliffe was a miserable time for her, too.

It was a tough time for all my family in fact. My dad works abroad a lot so being left in charge of the house was a pretty daunting prospect for him. He took my accident and the reality of me never walking again very hard and his personality is very different to Mum's so he was less able to hide his feelings for my sake and as a result was less hands-on during my time in hospital. It was still great to have him visit though, especially once I was in rehab. For a long time the only food I could stomach was sushi. He developed a routine of cycling over to the hospital around lunchtime and stopping on his way to pick up my daily fix. The nurses would let me sit up briefly to eat off the little table that swung over my bed and we'd chat about sport or the cards I'd received that day while I ate lunch. The boards around my bed were covered in cards that we arranged in a collage so it was a pretty nice place to be considering I was on the acute ward at a spinal injuries unit! He was always very vocal in his belief that I would walk again. I'll never forget him telling me that I could beat this and he'd be walking me down the aisle – like Mum and I he was all about the positive thinking. Dad is extremely protective of his family and it ate him up that there was nothing he could have done to prevent my accident, and his visions of my life from that point on were going to have to change.

It took a while even after I had finished rehab and was back at university for Dad to accept that I was going to be in a wheelchair for good, but once he did he became fully immersed in my athletics and knew my results better than I did. When I travelled abroad he followed my Twitter feed to find out how I did – I tend to be terrible at keeping my family updated – and would find the competition websites for every meet so he could track my results as they happened and sometimes stream my races. There were a few occasions when I was on a different continent to him and unable to find the race schedule or my results at a meet so texted him and got the desired information straight back faster than any of the race officials could even find it! A lot of my races took place in Switzerland, where Dad works a lot of the time, and they usually overlapped his birthday so I used to feel horribly guilty not seeing him on that day. In 2010 he solved that problem perfectly. He drove the three hours from Geneva, where he was working, to Lake Sempach, where I was racing an evening marathon, and made it there just in time to stand in the pouring rain for over two hours to watch my entire race, puncture and all, before driving straight back to Geneva to make it to work the next morning. After work the next day he then came all the way back to Sempach on his way to the Channel Tunnel to go for a belated birthday dinner with me and pick up my spare wheels so I didn't have to fly them home with me. He even offered to drive me home so I could get twelve hours of sleep before work the next morning rather than going through the usual rigmarole of flying with a racing chair.

My sister Fiona was only fourteen at the time of my accident and was in year ten at a small local school. My accident turned her summer upside down and I'm so grateful to her for the mature way in which she handled having to fit in around my parents' trips to hospital. My parents didn't want her to be too affected by what had happened to me so she had two days off school so that she could see me come out of my spinal surgery and then went back to class as normal. As naturally both my parents wanted to be able to visit me in those first days at the John Radcliffe she had to cope with being picked up by different friends. She was also required to take on a lot of responsibility at home alongside Mum's old friend Lois, who was a life-saver for keeping the horses looked after while Mum was in hospital with me. Fi never complained about the situation and it wasn't until over a year later that I found out how much it had affected her school life. For the final few weeks of the summer term after I broke my back she had a very tough time at school as her friends didn't know how to react.

A year later Fi changed schools and it was great for her to start afresh where people knew she had a disabled sister but didn't have any particular interest in bringing up what had happened to me. We're extremely close so I hated her having to deal with questions about my accident. She's still very protective of me and gets annoyed on my behalf when people treat me as though I have a mental disability or I can't get into a place that should really be wheelchair accessible. She's also my biggest supporter in her quiet way – she hardly ever says well done to me but when I was featured in *The Times* and when Sytner High Wycombe gave me my Mini she immediately put the photos up on Facebook.

After that first night beside my bed the ward sister told Mum she'd have to find a hotel or rent an apartment in Oxford if she wanted to be nearby as it was a hospital not a hotel! Being my mother she found a far better solution to the problem. As luck would have it, Stoke Mandeville NSIC happens to be close to my family home so the campaign to get me moved there began. As always with Mum she doesn't just get things done, she gets them done fast, so after five days I was told I'd be moving to Stoke Mandeville by the weekend. The day I got to move was a pretty momentous one. I was like a little kid going on holiday. As soon as I woke up we packed up all my things including the many cards and presents I'd received from my friends and family who came to visit. And we waited. And waited some more. Then the nurses came and informed us that there were no ambulances available that day. There was no way I was missing that miraculously found free bed at Stoke Mandeville so they found a private ambulance to take me on the extremely painful forty-minute journey between hospitals. Bizarrely, nobody had told the paramedics what was wrong with me so the drive was a little rocky until Mum pointed out that I'd just had spinal surgery! After that the driver was amazingly careful, avoiding the many potholes and speed bumps and dropping off the other patient who was sharing my ambulance as quickly as possible so that he could get me off the excruciatingly solid ambulance board and onto a hospital bed.

It was a massive relief to get out of that ambulance and through the doors of the NSIC. As I was pushed through reception to the lifts up to the wards I passed lots of people milling around in wheelchairs and I was surprised by how happy and relaxed they all looked. The reception area is very dark with a big pillar in the centre that had to be navigated, so I had plenty of time to sneak peeks at everyone. They smiled and waved back as though they were welcoming me into their home, not into a hospital. That's how Stoke Mandeville feels though – you're there for so long that it does start to feel like a home from home and it's the one hospital which doesn't give me that cold shudder when I go through its doors. Initially I was put on St Andrew's Ward, the acute ward where all new spinal injuries are taken. I was temporarily given my own room until I had been screened for MRSA and I even had a small wardrobe in which I could hang up some clothes. I refused to wear the hospital gowns for long so it quickly filled up with pyjamas, tracksuit bottoms and empire-line tops to hide how swollen the spinal surgery had made my torso. The nurses were so friendly and immediately told me off for lying on my back, which was great news as I'd hated being made to lie on it for a whole week at the John Radcliffe. I think that was probably the moment I decided I was a big fan of the NSIC, and I've stayed that way! As St Andrew's is on the top floor of the hospital I could look out of my window onto the occupational therapy garden. That first evening as I watched people in wheelchairs planting flowers alongside the occupational therapists in their green-and-white uniforms I actually felt quite excited about being in a place where my injury was in comparison fairly minor and where I could actually start my recovery.

3

Stoke Mandeville Hospital: Physical Rehab

It feels as though I'm spinning on the teacups at a theme park, my hands gripping the wheel in front of the seat and my weight being thrown into the side, except these teacups are on steroids. The world is spinning too fast and the ride is going on for too long, and I don't remember ever wanting to get on this ride in the first place. I don't feel fear or panic, just a total emptiness and unearthly sense of calm. Then the teacups turn into a rollercoaster as the view flips suddenly from blurred tarmac to a mixture of foliage and grass covering the glass that's now inches from my face. I try to move but I'm trapped by what feels like a dead weight pushing down on me so my lungs can't inflate and my legs won't move to get me out of there. The music has stopped and been replaced by a dull buzz inside my skull interrupted intermittently by a high-pitched bleeping sound. Gradually my eyes start to focus and I realize that the foliage in front of me is not in fact the branch that landed on my car windscreen when I crashed, but instead

19

the faded country-scene curtains around my hospital bed at the National Spinal Injuries Centre. It was just another flashback. Gradually the bleeping becomes less frantic as my heart rate slows, and I sit up and swing my legs off the bed.

Next thing I know I'm sitting on the floor with shooting pains up my recently pinned spine, having fallen rather abruptly out of bed. Of course now that I'm fully awake, thanks to my unplanned jolt from the floor, it all comes back. There was no dead weight stopping my legs from moving. They're paralysed and I'm never going to walk again. The feeling of frustration this brings (especially as I'm now a good three feet below the mattress I should be lying on with no way of getting up) is like a huge lump in my stomach trying to burst out and tears start to prick the back of my eyes. But there's no way I'm going to cry. I'm lucky to have the end bed on the ward, so I sit quietly for a few seconds straining for any hint that one of the nurses might have heard me bump to the ground, but thankfully there's nothing. As quietly as possible I brace my arms on the bed frame and the bedside locker and try to heave myself back onto the bed. Not happening. Maybe if I lower the bed that'll help. By now the frustration has been replaced by a weird sort of excitement at having a challenge to overcome as I stretch for the remote to bring the frame closer to the floor. Better. This time I can just about claw my way up and back onto the bed on my front as if I'm getting out of a swimming pool, and with the last of my rather lacking arm strength get my legs back under the sheets before the curtain rustles and Naomi, my favourite nurse, pops her head around the curtain.

'Everything all right, Nikki?'

'Yes, fine, thank you.'

'Ah, you bad girl – you mustn't lie on your back; you'll get a mark.'

She calls another nurse to help her flip me onto my side despite my protests that I'm more than capable of turning myself over (I don't mention that I just got myself up off the floor). As a newly injured patient with a large lump of metal holding my spine together I'm not supposed to move without a hideously constricting back brace so my escapades off the bed are probably best kept to myself!

'Lights off now my little girl?'

'Um, no it's fine – I think I'll read for a bit.'

No way am I risking another flashback to the crash that landed me in this strange acute ward where everyone thinks I'm incapable of raising an eyebrow without a team of nurses and physios on call. I'd rather read one of the many appalling self-help books well-meaning visitors have surrounded me with.

I was lucky to be moved to Stoke Mandeville NSIC only a week after my spinal surgery at the John Radcliffe. Often patients wait for months for a bed at a dedicated spinal unit, and some never receive the specialized care that a spinal unit brings. I'm sure that being able to complete all my recovery and rehabilitation at the NSIC played a big part in how quickly I was able to return to university and become involved in Paralympic sport.

The NSIC was the first hospital to introduce sport as part of the rehabilitation process after spinal injury under Sir Ludwig Guttmann's pioneering methodology. Guttmann had left Germany in 1939 after his Jewish roots made working in his professional role as a neurosurgeon impossible. He had been Medical Director of the Jewish Hospital in Breslau but after the Nazis began to show an interest in his activities as the hospital became a safe house for fleeing Jews, he managed to get away to Britain. He took a research post at the Radcliffe Infirmary in Oxford, working there and at the nearby St Hugh's Hospital. In 1941 he presented a review to the Medical Research Council of England on the treatment and rehabilitation of patients who had suffered a spinal cord injury which was to change the way in which spinal injuries were treated across Europe. Following this review the MRC decided to set up a dedicated centre for the treatment of spinal cord injuries at Stoke Mandeville Hospital as they expected the number of such injuries to rise during the attack of the second front in 1944. The twenty-six-bed centre was completed in 1943 and Guttmann became its Director under the proviso that he would have total control over the way in which patients were treated. The setting-up of a dedicated spinal injuries centre mirrored that established by Dr Munro at Boston City Hospital in 1936, and indeed many of Guttmann's therapeutic practices had their roots in Munro's methodology. Before such specialized treatment was available, spinal cord injury patients had a life expectancy of approximately two years after injury due to the dual threat of urinary tract infections and pressure sores. Although these issues can still be part of life as a wheelchair user they can easily be overcome in hospital by regular turning of patients and good hygiene, facts recognized by Munro and adopted by Guttmann.

From such humble beginnings the NSIC grew to a 200-bed unit under Guttmann's leadership and currently has plans to expand to include a full research facility. However much the hospital building and the technology inside it have changed, though, the ethos behind the care and rehabilitation of patients remains very similar to Guttmann's original philosophy. He stressed the importance of social rehabilitation as a result of his research into the psychological side of spinal cord injury, so patients were, and still are, encouraged to become independent as soon as possible after injury, play sport to encourage social interaction and spend time in the outside world during rehabilitation. These three things were, I believe, key to me being able to complete all the goals on the physiotherapists' and occupational therapists' checklists quickly enough to get back to university in time to start my third year with my friends.

At first I found the pressure to be independent difficult to keep up with during my time at the NSIC: I had to wear a horribly constricting back brace that ran from my chest to my hips with an additional piece coming up under my neck to give extra support to the metalwork placed around my spine during surgery after my accident. As I was going through rehabilitation during an uncharacteristically hot and sunny July and August for Britain, this was not only constrictive when breathing and obstructive when moving, but also uncomfortable and sticky in the heat. Wearing the brace meant I couldn't lean forward so it was difficult to learn how to transfer from one surface onto another using my arms during physiotherapy sessions as I was unable to redistribute my balance to lift myself up on my arms without falling forwards or backwards. This of course made being independent a struggle as without any power in my legs I had to use this transfer method for any movement into or out of my chair, from getting out of bed and going to the toilet, to sitting on a sofa and watching TV in the evening. I was given a sliding board, which effectively acts as a bridge between the wheelchair cushion and the surface you're aiming to sit on, allowing you to slide between the two, but after repeatedly trapping my hand under it and cutting my thumbs it was relegated to a cupboard and I learned to put my hands into fists to give me extra height for leverage and throw my weight sideways on one arm.

As a general rule I avoided the occupational therapy side of my rehabilitation timetable, preferring to participate just enough to get my box ticked so I was one step closer to getting out of hospital. The occupational therapists offered activities such as gardening, sewing, puzzles and painting but as far as I was concerned I didn't do those things as a walker and they weren't going to interest me any more now just because I was sitting down. I did enjoy the tests we had to complete to get that little box ticked, though. One task was to cook a meal for your occupational therapist and physio. By this point in my rehab I was already cooking my own meals to save my long-suffering mother from having to bring my dinner in every day as I was determined to eat healthily to help my body to heal rather than accepting the oil-drenched fried food on offer in the hospital canteen. As soon as I was strong enough to push back from the small parade of shops down the hill from the hospital I would go down there with fellow patients and buy my groceries while they picked up fish and chips for dinner. The kitchens at the hospital were so perfectly adapted for wheelchair users that it lulled me into a false sense of how easy cooking was going to be when I went back to university – they had lowered surfaces and cupboards, space under the sinks to wheel right up to them and pull-down baskets so you could even reach the top shelf. I had already made sticky toffee pudding for the physios with my friend Lena when she came to visit, so the meal was just a formality, but I really enjoyed getting the chance to cook pasta bake and toffee apple crumble for Susie, my occupational therapist, and Selina, my physio, as a thank-you for the time they'd invested in my recovery. I built a great relationship with both of them along with Georgie, the head of sport, and I still see them often five years after leaving Stoke Mandeville.

My consultant tried to keep me away from any team sports while I wore the back brace, so I would go to the old archery room, which had been the sports area at the NSIC since Guttmann's day, and do weights, archery and table tennis then hang around and watch the other patients play basketball every afternoon. Of course with my love of sports the watching didn't last and before long I was inventing wheelchair hockey with a group of similarly sporty inmates including a motocross rider, an oil-rig worker and an army parachute jumper. As with our games of basketball and even cricket this was a full-contact sport and our many falls out of the mixture of sports and everyday chairs we used gave us more opportunities to practise transfers than any physio session!

In addition to wheelchair sports I also had hydrotherapy sessions in the old pool down a wooden corridor from the physio gym. The room had windows on two sides and over the pool was a huge cumbersome hoist that could transfer patients from their everyday chair into the water. I didn't need the hoist for long as the sides of the pool were raised to make transferring directly from chair to pool easy. However, being pathetically immature I would try to persuade the hydrotherapy assistants to let me sit on the hoist and swing it over, then once I was above the water I'd push myself off so I could bomb into the pool. It didn't go down too well when there were other patients learning to float or being stretched by the side who got splashed! My swimming ability was quickly exploited by the lovely hydrotherapists; I would have a bungee strapped to my waist and be allowed to swim on the spot until I tired myself out and then be allowed to play with the foam floaties under the pretence of 'stretching'. It was a win–win situation as it meant I got the hang of swimming without legs very fast and so was quickly able to move into the 'big' pool at the nearby stadium to swim on my own, and it gave the hydrotherapists a much-needed break from lifting patients in the water!

At Stoke Mandeville the physiotherapy department tries hard to match patients to the physiotherapist who will best click with them. All of the physios at the NSIC that I met were lovely so I'm sure that whoever had been assigned to me would have been great but I'm really glad I got Selina. She's one of the most incredibly kind and patient people I've ever met, but also tons of fun and wouldn't take any rubbish from me. She'd also been to a school that I used to play lacrosse against so we had that in common. It's surprisingly common for spinal injuries patients to marry their physios/nurses/occupational therapists, which often comes as a surprise to people outside of the spinal injuries 'community'. You might expect that the last person you'd want to spend your life with would be someone who had such close knowledge of you at a time when you're learning how to do things a child finds simple, such as dress yourself or pick something up off the floor. In reality, though, the bond a lot of patients develop with hospital staff is very strong as they are effectively teaching you how to put your life back together. I still see Selina now that we've both left Stoke Mandeville, and I wish she was closer so I could see more of her. Alongside Selina, Georgie, who runs the sports department at the NSIC, became a close friend during my time in rehab and we still catch up for tea regularly. In addition I'm constantly bumping into her when I'm working out at Stoke Mandeville Stadium and she is running sports sessions for patients there, and it's not unheard of for me to join in a game of wheelchair hockey or a wheelchair skills session. Despite her best efforts while I was an inpatient my kerb-jumping skills are still embarrassingly non existent so I need all the extra help I can get! I like chatting to the newly injured patients she's in charge of too as they all have interesting stories to tell and I hope that maybe talking to me and seeing someone who's happy being in a wheelchair might inspire some of the ones who are having a harder time adjusting to their new life.

3 a.m.: The day the woman in the bed next to me leaves this ward will be my happiest of the last month. I know the physios told her to stretch her legs every three hours as she's learning to walk but I'm confident they didn't mean in the middle of the night! If only the nurses would leave my wheelchair near my bed, I'd sneak over and turn off that stupid alarm clock to give us all an undisturbed night's sleep.

4 a.m.: Brilliant – incompetent woman number two in the bed opposite me has decided she needs some water. Cue the nurse alarm being pulled. They're waking us up in two hours anyway – just be thirsty!

5 a.m.: Oh, for the love of God! Could the woman on the end not cry quietly?! Right, no point even trying to get back to sleep now – in one hour the nurses will be waking everyone up anyway. This is a pretty good opportunity to grab an hour reading Lance Armstrong's autobiography – I won't get much chance the rest of the day.

6.30 a.m.: Sure enough, the curtains around my bed have been thrown open. Now it's time to try to barter a shower out of the nurses. I got one yesterday but I have lots of friends visiting today and I want the ones who haven't seen me in my chair yet to at least see me with clean hair. Sadly, with this stupid back brace I'm not allowed to sit up in the shower so I have to wait for a nurse to push me into the wet room on the waterproof bed, and none of them seem too keen.

8 a.m.: Still no shower and I have physio in half an hour. I guess it'll be a dry-shampoo day.

8.30 a.m.: Today we're learning to build blocks and throw beanbags in physio. No joke – I have to totally relearn how to sit up without something to lean against as my centre of balance needs to be directly over my hips or I'll topple over, having no abdominal or back muscles to keep me stable. So Selina and I throw beanbags to each other and I stack paper cups. Often I fall forwards onto the bench or backwards into the foam wedge but I think I'm improving . . . slowly! We also try some split-level transfers but without being able to lean forward too far in the back brace they're pretty unsuccessful.

10 a.m.: I love the physios. Someone missed their hydrotherapy so I've been allowed to take their slot . . . which means shower*!*

10.20 a.m.: After twenty minutes of swimming attached to the bungee belt so I don't have to keep turning around every length I finally get my shower as there are no nurses around by the pool to tell me I can't sit up.

10.25 a.m.: In hindsight it might have been better to master those split-level transfers before trying to get from my day chair onto the shower stool. Going via the floor wasn't part of the plan!

10.45 a.m.: Up to Jimmy's café for tea with Mum. She comes in every day. I'm so lucky to live so close and have such a great mum!

12 p.m.: Yay, my friends have arrived! As usual Lou is here and today Ceci, Rose, Izzie, Emma and Ramsay have joined her. Ramsay's teaching me the guitar but so far I'm not a great pupil – I'd rather be down in the archery room playing sport than *practising music! They've brought with them a feast of all my favourite foods so we head outside using my lap as a shopping trolley to carry the bags while Rose pushes me (the only time I'll let anyone do that!). She nearly throws me out of the chair by ramming me first into a door frame and then into a small step. Good job I can't feel my legs!*

2 p.m.: After approximately 5000 Percy Pigs I really can't miss fitness class so I head down to the archery room with Ramsay where I do laps, along with a bunch of the other sporty patients, with spinning and slalom interspersed. I'm still a bit of a learner driver so I really think Georgie has it in for me in these sessions!

3 p.m.: Now it's basketball time. Actually I hate basketball as I'm incapable of shooting hoops so after a few minutes of playing with all the patients and Ramsay we manage to persuade Georgie that hockey's a much better sport. So a full-on contact grudge match of wheelchair hockey ensues. As usual Alex tips his chair over backwards, Andy falls out forwards and I smash my thumb almost as much as I smash other people's with my stick.

5 p.m.: This is when the day gets a little dull if you don't have visitors so it's great to see my sister after she's finished school. She's actually got an ulterior motive for the visit but I'm happy to help with her biology homework in exchange for a couple of hours with her.

6.30 p.m.: Awesome surprise – I thought Dad would just come and pick Fi up but instead he and Mum have both arrived with a noodle-bar take away! Not strictly part of my 'spinal-cord regeneration' list of foods but they don't seem to be working so I'm pretty happy to get my carton of sticky chilli beef and rice.

9 p.m.: Now I'm exhausted. I don't know if it's the drugs, the exercise or the lack of sleep in the early hours of the morning but I'm dead by the end of every day.

9.30 p.m.: Perfect timing to get back to my ward – the nurses are bringing around hot drinks so I can grab a hot chocolate while I get another chapter of Lance in. Not that I'll manage a full chapter when I'm this tired.

4

Social Rehab

As is probably evident, I was quick to overcome any challenges that could be beaten by physical strength or a little rule bending. What I really struggled with was the social rehabilitation side of my new situation. Having been so image conscious before breaking my back I lost a lot of confidence being in a wheelchair. I felt unattractive as a consequence both of not being able to walk and of putting on a stone and a half while not able to move during bed rest and my time in the back brace. I hated people seeing me in my chair. When all but my closest friends came to visit I'd try and be in bed until the nurses spotted what I was doing and banned me from being in bed during the day. Somehow being in bed made it seem as though I was any ill person you might visit in hospital whereas when I was up in my chair it made my disability a permanent reality. Looking back, this is probably something I should have discussed with Dr

Paul Kennedy, the renowned clinical psychologist I was required to see every week and who went on to supervise my dissertation. However, in my strong-willed way I was convinced I was totally fine mentally and did not need to see a psychologist and therefore discussed as little as possible with him.

My psychology sessions were not how I expected them to be having studied psychology for two years by that point. I thought I was far too knowledgeable to be 'fooled' by this psychologist who thought he could 'trick' me into divulging my secrets. Most of the psychology I'd studied used psychometric testing so I thought I'd be doing lots of this and could work out what Dr Kennedy was trying to get me to reveal and answer the questions in such a way as to avoid that. At first I did have to do a couple of tests but they were so long and seemingly random that I ended up having to answer truthfully as I couldn't figure out which of the options would make me seem the least depressed or affected by my accident. I'm not sure if the results told him anything really but I suppose going through the painful process of getting me to agree to do them showed him my attitude towards having to see a psychologist. As our sessions wore on though I actually started looking forward to sitting in Paul's cramped office upstairs in the NSIC once a week and being able to tell him anything without worrying that he'd get upset or think that I wasn't coping as I did with my friends and family. He would start out asking how my week had been and I'd give him a long rundown of all the things I'd achieved in physio and sport. He was quick to praise my physical progress but also firm in forcing me to go deeper than that surface look at how I was doing that I always gave him.

Paul worried that I was using sport and the other activities available at the hospital to fill my time so that I didn't have to think about my predicament, so he tried to encourage me to sit and plan what I wanted to do after I left hospital. Looking back I don't think it would have been a bad thing if I'd listened to him, but I don't think sport was just a way for me to hide from the reality of being disabled during my time in rehab. I had always been sporty so continuing with that was my way of holding on to the one thing that hadn't changed in my life and using that to get the rest of my world turned upright again. Had I not played sport I would have dwelled on all the items on my list of the twenty-five things I wanted to do before I died that I couldn't do, rather than realizing that actually with a bit of work I could probably do most of them and those that I couldn't manage in a wheelchair (e.g. the Marathon des Sables) could be replaced by equally exciting things that I was still capable of doing.

Once we'd got through the easy stuff, and I'd described pretty much every transfer of the week in detail to Paul in order to put off the inevitable difficult questions, we moved on to how I was coping. For a few weeks I refused to admit that the wheelchair was permanent as I was determined I could make myself walk if I worked hard enough and ate enough kale and sushi. Then, during one session, Paul wouldn't let me leave until I'd said I wasn't going to walk.

And meant it. I was furious and sat in silence as he spelled it out to me. I can still hear his Irish accent saying, *'You. Are. Not. Going. To. Walk.'*

'But Selina said I can have callipers made to support my legs so I can walk on them.'

'Nikki, that is not walking. Callipers are not a viable method of moving around over any distance for you and you would need to use crutches to support yourself. Within a few months you would damage your shoulders. You have a complete spinal injury and at this time a wheelchair is your only option.'

'I might get my legs back though. The journals say spinal shock can last up to eight weeks, so my spinal cord might just be in shock still.'

'That's very unlikely as you have no movement or feeling below your injury level, but even if something does come back it is unrealistic to expect you will have enough movement to walk. You will still be a wheelchair user.'

'It's only temporary, though. Stem cell research has been approved and there's a place called the XCell-Center in Germany that already does stem cell therapy on spinal injury patients.'

'Nikki, if that therapy was a legitimate cure for spinal injury do you not think it would be carried out in more than one centre?'

We had many conversations like the one above where I would argue from every angle that my current wheelchair use was only a temporary glitch and Paul would calmly and politely shut down my protests. Eventually, though, he got the quivering, tentative reply he had been looking for: 'I know I'm not going to walk again.'

After that our sessions became more relaxed and we'd

chat generally about how I felt about being disabled. In many ways getting through that first hurdle of giving up hope of walking made the wheelchair a lot easier to accept and pushed me to try even harder in physio and sports sessions, as if this was my new life I was damn well going to be the best at it. Looking back I really just treated using a wheelchair as a new sport to learn but it was a good method for me as I stopped thinking of it as an unwanted imposter in my life.

After a month or so I was totally comfortable talking to Paul and we'd often have our chats out in the garden. I struggled mentally after my then boyfriend broke up with me so my counselling sessions with Paul focused on that for a while. Being newly single was almost as hard to deal with as being in a wheelchair but, thankfully, the rugby-playing Build-a-Bear named Lawrence (after Dallaglio) my friend Murray brought me kept me company!

One day Miss Collier, my old housemistress, popped in to visit and joined Paul and I in the occupational therapy garden. Totally unperturbed by my saying I was in the middle of a psychology session she pulled up a bench and brought out three cups of tea. She told Paul what I'd been like at school so I guess at least it gave him some further character insight! My consultant had to get used to my never-ending stream of visitors, too. Mr Derry did ward rounds every Tuesday and if I had close friends or family visiting they would sit in on my check-up and even ask questions. Lou became especially well versed on my routines and recovery once Mr Derry gave up trying to keep my details personal when I was quite obviously so relaxed about them being shared with my friends. At first he and I didn't see eye to eye as he took a while to realize that, thanks to my studying for a neuroscience degree, he couldn't fob me off with just basic information and I was determined to be as involved as possible in my recovery. In particular I wanted to come off some of the twenty-eight tablets I was on daily but he wouldn't let me. So I found out what each one did, decided on the ones I thought I didn't need, namely anything designed to prevent pain or depression, and stopped taking them. Then I demanded to be allowed to go home for a few hours to get away from the claustrophobia of the ward even though I was still newly injured and in a back brace. I wasn't exactly the ideal patient but now Mr Derry and I get on really well and he's always brilliant at answering any questions I have and solving any problems that are having an impact on my ability to live as though I'm not disabled. One time I called his secretary about having internal Botox, as he'd recommended at my yearly check-up, to tell her that I was going away in a week for athletics so the operation would have to wait until I got back, but she called back that afternoon saying they'd squeezed me in for the next day and asked how quickly I could get to the hospital! I think that highlights the continuing support Stoke Mandeville NSIC staff give to their ex-patients.

When my best school friends came to visit it was a different matter being in my chair. The dream team of Rose, Izzie, Ceci, Lou and Ramsay made me feel totally comfortable and even forget about the chair, and it would actually be them trying to get me to sit on my bed so they could play in my wheelchair. They even came to my physio and sports sessions with me on the pretence of learning how they could help me, but I'm pretty sure they just wanted to play with the beanbags I had to practise throwing to improve my balance and have a go at wheelchair basketball. Ramsay in particular was very good at treating us new wheelchair users just as he would anyone else on a sports field – with aggression and competitiveness. He got pretty good at wheelchair basketball and made no allowances for those of us without the balance to match his skill! Even Rose's mother had a go at wheelchair skills. The positive attitude everyone who visited me had to wheelchair sport definitely played a big part in my enthusiasm for it. Not once did anyone behave as though sport in a wheelchair was a lesser version of the able-bodied counterpart, so choosing what I wanted to focus on once I left rehab wasn't so much choosing a disabled sport, it was just picking a new activity. Even now my friends ask to try out my racing chair but as my legs have lost so much mass from not being used it's a bit of a tight squeeze for them to fit into the kneeling seat. My everyday chair is still fair game as soon as I get out of it though!

I was lucky in that my friends and family dropped everything to spend a huge amount of time at the hospital with me so I felt a bit like a queen getting to hold court and have everyone come to her. I probably saw more of any of my friends than I would have had I been at home! My family were worried about going on their planned summer holiday and leaving me, but in reality my friends were more than happy to step into the gap and take up pretty much permanent residence in Jimmy's café at the NSIC. Because of this I wasn't really part of the cliques that had grown up among the other patients, especially as most were a lot older than me. There was one particularly raucous group of older men who called themselves 'G-Block' and turned their time in rehab into one big party. That's what was particularly strange about being in St Joseph's Ward (the independent ward you moved to a month before being discharged) – by that point the patients weren't ill so the atmosphere reminded me of the dorms at school with the camaraderie between patients and the nurses taking the place of housemistresses. Whenever my friends left I'd be inundated with questions from the guys about my hot friends! Once the pain in my back had started to ease that summer actually felt more like a summer camp full of sports and socializing than a stay in hospital. Of course I was constantly learning new things in physio every morning that would enable me to be independent back at uni but the rest of the day was pretty much mine to fill as I pleased. It made it very easy to forget that all too soon I'd have to face the real world where not everything was accessible and not everyone was knowledgeable and accepting about people in wheelchairs.

One of my closest friends from Oxford, Lena, was studying at Yale University during the summer I broke my back so by the time she could make it back to the UK I was already nearing the end of my rehabilitation time and was on St Joseph's Ward. I don't know whether it was not having seen me in the acute stage after my injury when I was unable to even push a wheelchair that played a part in her attitude to me after the accident or her childhood brush with serious illness and long-standing propensity for serious injury that made her even more accepting of the situation than my school friends had been. After the first few visits all my friends stopped asking how I felt or whether I was OK about not walking again, but Lena never really asked at all. On her first visit to the hospital, bringing with her our favourite cupcakes and Percy Pigs, she behaved as though she was popping over to my house for tea and was totally au fait with all the parts of being in a wheelchair that people don't think about, such as having to catheterize to go to the bathroom and needing drugs to be able to digest food. Until I saw her I'd been worried about how the friends I went out clubbing with at university would react to me being in a chair but after seeing Lena I stopped worrying about going back once I left Stoke Mandeville.

She was shocked to see me dressed in sweats and a baggy T-shirt with split ends in my hair and no make-up and was quite happy to call me out on it. In hospital that's all anyone in chairs wore so I'd got into the habit of living in leggings or tracksuit bottoms. Jeans were quite tough to get on at first and pumps didn't stay on my feet so I gave up and dressed like a slob. That didn't last once Lena was back in the country, though! I'll never forget her stepping back once she'd given me a selection of gorgeous gifts from the States and lots of hugs and saying, totally aghast, *'Sweetie what are you wearing?!'*

'I have physio and sport all day so it makes sense to wear sweats around the hospital.'

'That does not mean you need to look like this.'

So I rediscovered my GHDs, dug out my bronzer and asked Mum to bring some of my proper clothes to Stoke Mandeville. Embarrassingly, though, the first thing I asked Baroness Tanni Grey-Thompson, the eleven-time Paralympic gold medallist wheelchair racer, when I met her at the Paralympic handover party on the day of the Beijing Paralympic closing ceremony at Stoke Mandeville Stadium was how she got into a pair of jeans! Since then I've become very adept at wiggling my lifeless legs into the tightest of non-stretchy skinny jeans. Definitely the most useful skill I've learned! Along with Lou and my close friend from university, Jodie, Lena was one of the people who made possible my return to Oxford only four days after I got out of hospital and got me through the mental side of no longer being able to run around the city as I used to. She was also the driving force behind me losing the hospital weight as fast as possible so I could get back into my bodycon dresses!

Once the back brace was off I was allowed to leave the hospital for a few hours, so Mum took me home. I was shocked at how much being in such familiar surroundings but in such an unfamiliar situation upset me and I was desperate to get back to the hospital. I tried to pretend to enjoy being able to curl up on the sofa and have tea and cake with my family, but actually the effort it had taken to get me out of the car and into the house exhausted and embarrassed me and I couldn't imagine how I could ever be anything but a burden on my friends and family. After the bubble of the NSIC where I could get around everywhere and be totally independent, the real world was a nasty surprise. It was great to meet the builders who were converting the outbuilding opposite my parents' barn into a studio apartment for me and work on the plans, though. We decided it would be open plan with just the bathroom walled off and I couldn't wait to see how it looked with the internal walls removed.

Soon after the trip home, my godmother came to visit and took me to the Woolpack, a great gastropub up the road from the hospital with wooden beams and a cosy, welcoming atmosphere inside. Being so close to the spinal unit the staff were used to being inundated with patients in chairs; the restaurant was totally accessible with squishy seats that I could easily transfer into and my confidence in my ability to live a normal life after being discharged started to return. Then I noticed how much the other clients were looking at me. Before my accident I'd sometimes get attention from guys when I was out but this was totally different – people were openly staring. At first I worried my salad had got stuck in my teeth. Then I thought maybe I'd accidentally had a Bridget Jones moment with my bronzer. And finally it dawned on me that it was the wheelchair that made grown men and women feel it was acceptable to openly stare at someone trying to have a quiet lunch with a friend. I suppose it was good to experience this in such a closed setting before I ventured out into town on one of my home visits, as being stared at in a shopping centre was even more disconcerting. People would almost walk into each other they were so busy looking at my wheels rather than their path. Still, I'm glad I had the chance to experience the reaction of strangers to my disability while I was still in hospital, and so could return to the friends I'd made in rehab and laugh about what strange treatments we'd received in the outside world that day. It allowed me to gradually acclimatize. The reactions can be just as bad now but I try to tell myself that people are just surprised to see someone so young and otherwise normal-looking in a wheelchair and make myself smile brazenly at their confused faces. If I'm having a slightly down day, though, it's difficult to see the furtive glances and open gazing in this positive light. It's much easier to assume they stare because they think you're a freak.

Another hurdle to overcome before you can be declared ready to leave the NSIC is a weekend away from the hospital. I was determined to prove I could do this as I'd already missed so many of my friends' twenty-first birthday parties and wanted to be allowed to go to the last few of the summer. The first I was allowed to attend was my friend Ed's. This was a fairly simple challenge – Dad would drive me to the dinner in London then pick me up and take me home to sleep. What was less simple was the flight of stone church stairs down to the crypt where the restaurant was housed at the edgy venue Ed had chosen, the flight of stairs up to the bathroom and the lack of accessibility to said bathroom once I'd made it up there. Everyone was so lovely carrying my chair and me up and down the stairs but I felt like such a hindrance to all my friends that, as great as it was to see them, I wished I hadn't gone. Spending the night at home also proved to be less than ideal as I found it difficult to transfer onto my bed, which had been moved into the downstairs sitting area, as it was so much lower than the hospital beds. However, I had to get through that night as a couple of weeks later I had a far more difficult trial to overcome.

I wanted to get a lift with friends from uni to our friend Rafi's twenty-first and there was no way my consultant or my parents would let that happen unless I pretended to have breezed through Ed's. As it happens I probably should have admitted to myself that I wasn't yet ready to be back in my old social circle partying all night. I was still getting to grips with being in a chair and my transfers and wheelchair skills weren't reliable enough to allow me to get around inaccessible places or be as independent as I am now. Rafi had put ramps up everywhere but I didn't have the strength to get up the steep gradients. Having done stairs in my wheelchair skills classes I decided to take them on after far too many glasses of Rafi's famous Midori cocktail, and of course ended up on the floor. Having such great friends there helped so much, though, and I didn't mind asking for help as I had at Ed's – I guess I was getting used to needing the occasional lift or shove. What did affect me was seeing everyone dancing. In my opinion dancing in a wheelchair is nothing like the same as dancing when you can use your legs and I find it embarrassing to watch and to do. It's one of the few things I still really miss, especially as it was such a big part of my pre-accident life since I worked at a nightclub.

Despite my minor psychological wobble at Rafi's twenty-first, the nurses and physios deemed my weekends away a success and they declared me fit to leave with a discharge date four days before term started at Oxford. It was cutting it fine but I'd spent a day in the city with Susie, my occupational therapist, earlier in the summer to make sure I'd be able to get around once I went back, so everything was in place well before I left hospital. The first thing we did was to drive past the place where I had crashed, and as I pointed it out to Susie I was surprised that I felt nothing. Or at least I thought I'd pointed it out. About 400 m further up the road we came to a point where the trees were disturbed and skid marks were still visible on the grass. Just goes to show how much of an effect the accident must have had on me psychologically – despite all my hated flashbacks I hadn't even remembered where it had happened! Now that the trees have grown over again I honestly couldn't say exactly where it was but whenever I drive from Headington to north Oxford along the ring road I go very slowly and carefully down that whole stretch!

After the 'drive past' was complete we had a long list of places to check out for access. First we went to Magdalen College, where I'd been studying for the past two years. My main concern about access there was that I'd been top of the room ballot for my final year so I had first choice of room and had picked the most idyllic spot in the New Building (which is actually very old) overlooking the deer park and the lawns. I was pretty determined that if they weren't going to let me bum up the stairs in order to keep that room the alternative had to be pretty special! It was. Mark Blandford-Baker, the Home Bursar of the college whom I had got to know through my time on the Commemoration Ball Committee, showed us through to the accessible room in Grove Quad and it was a pretty good replacement for my dream room. I would have a bedroom and sitting room that overlooked the deer park on three sides and a big bathroom that they were prepared to adapt to Susie's exact specifications. I only had one request: there were alarm cords everywhere and I wanted them gone! Magdalen also ramped the step from the car park and gave me a prime parking space so that later I could drive to and from some of my further-away lectures when the weather was bad, and also to and from Iffley Road gym. So we knew I'd have somewhere suitable to live on my return, which was a relief as the building work required to give me a bedroom at my parents' house was running behind schedule and once I left hospital I would not be able to shower in my new room there.

Next we went to the Science Park where the majority of my lectures and tutorials took place. Knowing how old the buildings around Oxford are I didn't hold out much hope for the psychology and physiology lecture halls but I was pleasantly surprised to discover that there were lifts that could get me to a lot of the rooms. It's amazing how much of my surroundings I'd never noticed as I rushed to and from lectures and sports practices. The staff in the physiology and psychology departments could not have been more helpful in their drive to allow me to finish my degree as I'd always intended. Any lectures for the options I'd selected that were in rooms I couldn't get to were moved to the Medical Sciences Teaching Centre and pharmacology building, which were new and fully accessible. I decided I didn't want to battle with lab work as I was unsure of my balance, being so newly injured, so they allowed me to switch to a non-lab option with no fuss. Once I was actually back at university I was even more pleasantly surprised by how many of my lecturers offered to move tutorials closer to Magdalen or into larger rooms for my benefit.

A lot of people I meet in wheelchairs who are applying for university cross Oxbridge off their list before they even start, not for academic reasons but because they wrongly assume that they won't be able to get around. Yes, there are cobbles in both Oxford and Cambridge. And yes, a lot of rooms are up flights of stairs, especially at the older colleges like Magdalen, which made my final year less fun than I'd hoped. But it is totally possible to study at Oxford or Cambridge if you are in a wheelchair, and with all the improvements the colleges are making you can even get into the bar and junior common room if you choose the right one. The Iffley Road Sports Complex is currently being redeveloped, too, so there will be a top-class accessible sports facility at Oxford University in the next few years.

When the time finally came for me to leave Stoke Mandeville NSIC on the afternoon of 26 September 2008, to say I was apprehensive would be a massive understatement. I spent the morning running through the final checklists with my physio and occupational therapist to check that I was as fully prepared for going out into the world in a chair as the hospital required. Then Lena arrived, bringing with her our friend Arthur, from whom I had been inseparable throughout second year, as we were on the same course and both worked at The Oxford Retreat pub and ran the FTSE@Filth club night. It was great to see him.

Along with Arthur, Lena had brought cupcakes and my mum provided champagne, so my final sports session that afternoon was a great celebration. After eleven long weeks it was time to go home for a few days before returning to university, settling back into life in the outside world from a slightly lower vantage point. It didn't really hit until Mum and I got home that this really was my new reality. I went up the temporary metal ramp into the kitchen and had a cup of tea with all my family. Then I just felt empty. In hospital it had been easy to forget that I wasn't just on a summer course where I got to play wheelchairs for a while. I was never going to walk again. And I had to go back to uni in a few days in a bulky, ugly wheelchair as my permanent one wouldn't be ready for a few weeks. How could this be my future? My final year was supposed to be full of Commemoration Balls and punting and garden parties, not wheelchairs and catheters and hospital checks. Of course it didn't take long to discover that these two alternatives are not mutually exclusive but those first few hours after being discharged from hospital were pretty scary. I felt totally lost and unsure of what to expect on my return to university a few days later.

The upside was that my new studio apartment had nearly been completed opposite my parents' barn. It is the perfect building for a wheelchair user to live in as the door is not full-sized and once you duck inside the beams are at head-bumping height for anyone standing up. I couldn't sleep in there yet as there was no electricity or running water but the walls had been painted pale cream and the dark-wood-effect floor Mum and I had picked out a few weeks before my release from hospital had been laid. The bathroom was also finished, complete with black-and-white chequerboard tiles in the shower and backlit mirror. We'd measured everything at the hospital to make sure that the height of the sink and toilet were ideal for me to reach and transfer onto and the entire floor was tiled with black slate so my wheels wouldn't damage it if they got wet. With the addition of bright pink towels and soaps it was, and still is, a bathroom fit for any five-star hotel! The best bit was that once it was finished it meant I could finally wash at home rather than having to be driven to Stoke Mandeville Stadium to use the showers there as I'd had to do on my weekends out of hospital.

As we knew I would only have a few days at home before returning to Oxford there was no rush to get the kitchen put into my studio. I'd picked it out in preparation for my return at the end of term, though. The kitchens at the hospital had been very easy for me to cook in so we used the same company that had installed them to do mine, albeit on a far smaller scale. As the studio is fairly small the kitchen needed to fit along one wall perpendicular to the bathroom and finish with enough space for me to fit a sofa in before the wardrobe. The designers did a great job, creating a granite-topped surface with white wooden cupboards housing the fridge and freezer that tied into the cabinet where I would store all my books to one side and more cupboards above. The hob has empty space below so I can get my legs under to allow me to reach the pans on the back burner and the sink is lower than in a normal kitchen, which makes washing up easier. The little additions they came up with, such as having a pull-out shelf below the oven so I didn't put hot dishes on my lap and pull-down shelves in the cupboards so I could reach things on the top shelf, have made the whole kitchen much easier to use; it was definitely worth getting specialists in to design the area. Moving out after finishing university definitely brought home just how perfect my little studio had been, and how easy it made life!

In addition to having the kitchen specially designed to be accessible for me we also thought through all the fittings for the other areas of the studio very carefully in order to use the space in the best way possible. With my first chair being quite cumbersome I needed a lot of space to open doors, so we decided that with the exception of the bathroom and the kitchen cupboards we wouldn't put doors on anything. Instead I chose a great set of fabrics in wide stripes of cream with either pastel pink, blue or yellow. We used the yellow to make curtains to go around the wardrobe and chest of drawers, the blue for window blinds and all three for cushions for my cream sofa. I then added wicker baskets to divide up storage areas and all in all it looked so beautiful I didn't want to leave to go back to Oxford.

In the years since my accident my parents have replaced the gravel drive between my studio and their barn, and put a permanent paved ramp up to the door of their house. They also added a car port where Millie, my Mini Clubman, now lives. I've now moved into a flat in London which is pretty good as Fulham accessibility goes, yet still has nothing on my old studio. When I go home to visit my parents I love being able to curl up in my little studio and have everything I need right beside me. After a long week that's pretty much a bed, a duvet and the TV remote! The barn where the rest of my family live being so inaccessible and inadaptable due to its listed status has definitely worked out in my favour.

5

Oxford University

5.30 p.m., Thursday, Trinity Term, 2008, Pharmacology Building, University of Oxford

Six weeks and counting until the second-year Part I Physiology exams start and I'm sitting at the back of a neuroscience lecture between my friends Lena and Arthur looking every inch the dedicated Oxbridge student with my books and highlighters. Another close friend, Guy, sits in front of us with his back turned to the screen where a doctorate student is getting excited about sound location in the brain. In front of me is a handout with multi coloured notes scribbled around the miniature replicas of the slides that have been flashing up for the past thirty minutes. Unfortunately all of us lost track somewhere around slide 250, so the density of scribbles somewhat peters out part way down the page. I'm not too worried, though – since I'd decided fairly early on in the year that the auditory system wasn't going to be one of my selected themes for finals, I'm only attending this lecture because it's a good place to go over the final details for tonight's Trinity Term launch of

FTSE@Filth, the club night Arthur and I took over in our second year at Oxford.

In three and a half hours Lena and I will be working on the door of Filth, an aptly named club above a car park in the main Oxford shopping centre, dressed in Primark bikinis and suit shirts. Not a standard wardrobe choice for a Thursday night! Glancing out the window for a moment across Lena's Thailand-acquired enviably golden skin at the torrential downpour I start to wish we could just go back to last term's City theme . . . my well-worn shot-girl uniform suddenly seems a whole lot more appealing than the white bikinis we'd picked up for all the girls on our way to this lecture. Still, that cute dress in the Karen Millen window will more than make up for five hours of holding my stomach in and smiling through gritted teeth, and if tonight goes well I'll earn enough to pay for that along with matching shoes and a week's rent. Finally, movement on the bench in front signals it's time for Lena and I to shove the neglected notes into our handbags (avoiding smudging my still-wet glossy red nails) and use our lacrosse-induced running abilities to get out of there as fast as possible before half the students accost us, looking for free entry or a queue jump that night. It's funny how many 'friends' you gain when you've got the ear of the Oxford bouncers!

Leaving Lena at New College on the way to my house with promises that this time I'll be ready when she comes to pick me up (I won't), I jog into Harvey's to pick up dinner . . . if an apple can be called dinner! Bikini+food baby=not very attractive shot girl. Then the best bit of the night starts – getting ready with the girls! Due to my poorly stocked iTunes my friend Jodie's room, a few houses away from mine, is the venue of choice and within half an hour her room resembles the backstage area at a catwalk show walked by alcoholics, with make-up, multiple GHDs, bottles of Oddbins Own, discarded clothes and accessories on every surface. When Lena arrives looking infuriatingly elegant in the dreaded white bikini and denim mini with her hair beautifully curled I'm hopping around in a bikini top, Oxford Lacrosse trackies, one pink heel and one strappy gold stiletto that I can't undo the buckle of, with only one eye made up. But I'm pretty proud of myself – this is comparatively prepared considering my normal train-wreck state ten minutes before we're due to go out!

Although having to arrive at Filth by 9 p.m., hours before anyone in their right mind would be thinking about going clubbing, has its drawbacks (such as cutting down preparation time so drastically that I was forced to walk down the High Street with half-done make-up and an unbeatably chavtastic combination of trackies and heels) there are some definite positives: an empty dance floor complete with a DJ who will play all our requests; getting to play in the ball pit we create every week in the VIP area before the masses arrive and it becomes more like a rugby pitch; and, most importantly tonight, empty bathrooms with mirrors available to finish off my make-up. Once the crowds start to arrive Arthur, Lena and I will be flat out running the door; making sure we retain capacity for pre-booked groups such as sports teams and crew dates, stopping fights breaking out in the queue, or even worse people leaving the queue; and pouring shots into open mouths on the dance floor. Thanks to Serge the cocktail barman it's not all work and no play, though, as his complimentary mudslides and lemon drops are enough to keep us smiling all night and with the many shots of tequila friends keep buying me it doesn't seem long before the Grease *soundtrack's playing and the lights start to come up at the end of the six-hour shift.*

It's easy to forget that the night's about work not play once we've stopped letting people in but as soon as the clients leave that soon changes. In my opinion there are few places less attractive than a club after closing time. The bright lights reveal sticky floors and peeling walls, and the ball pit no longer looks like a fun place to play but rather the balls seem to be floating in a suspicious amount of dirty liquid at the bottom of which is a veritable treasure trove of watches, phones and room keys. With the help of the bar staff we soon get all 10,000 brightly coloured plastic balls into their bin bags for storage.

By the time I've collected my cut of the door takings and made it out of the club it's well past 4 a.m. and the knowledge that I have to be up in two and a half hours to get to lacrosse fitness training is not welcome. What is welcome, though, is my friend leaning on the wall of the shopping centre holding a spare hoodie and foam containers of chips, with a can of Diet Coke in his pocket. As the temperature is now well below ten degrees and all I've eaten since lunch is an apple, nothing could make me happier than these! Oxford isn't the nicest place to walk through at night and having someone there makes me feel a lot safer crossing the city to get home, not to mention the bonus of added body heat to counteract the chill.

It's not long until sunrise and there's only one place to watch that from if you're a Magdalen student – the roof of the houses on the High Street. It's a bit of a climb to get out there and as usual I make a very unladylike showing, squeezing through the gap in the bars above the bath. Once I'm out I wait to be shown the route up the tiles holding on to the chimneys and drains to get to the top of the slope. With the earlier rain everything's a bit slippery and I keep tripping but managing to catch hold of something to stop myself crashing down onto the High Street below. It's worth the cuts and grazes, though, once I make it up and sit looking down over the city with a great friend beside me as the sun rises above what must be one of the most beautiful skylines in Britain . . . even if I will have to take on lacrosse practice after pulling an all-nighter.

After a quick shower to scrub off the layers of make-up and roof dirt it's time to go again, but this time in a less provocative outfit of trainers, green hockey socks, baggy blue shorts that lost all their shape at some point while I was at school but still form the centrepiece of my sportswear wardrobe, a Harvard University T-shirt I picked up while working at a summer camp in the US last summer and a borrowed Magdalen rugby shirt. The university parks are the opposite side of town to my house and the jog over there in the hazy early morning spring sunshine is perfect for clearing my head. By some miracle I've made it on time and the adrenaline and sugar rushing through my bloodstream after my dawn feast several stories up in the air are enough to get me through the barrage of sprints, drills and circuits despite the lack of sleep. By the end I don't think I'll make it all the way back to Magdalen, so I'm actually grateful for my 9 a.m. lecture in the medical sciences building adjacent to the park. It's the perfect place to dissect the previous night's events with Arthur and Guy and grab a quick nap between my turns at the Monopoly game we've been playing on Arthur's phone for as long as we've had lectures together!

Now that's over, and I've found the energy to make it down the million stairs from the top of the lecture hall to the exit, it's definitely time to wake Jodie up so she can fill me in on all the gossip I missed while I was working. Her room's also slightly closer to lectures than mine and at this point the greater proximity of her bed wins out and I can't wait to crash out there and spend the morning eating bacon sandwiches, drinking tea and watching chick flicks until lunchtime, when we can legitimately crack open the Pimm's and go punting in the sunshine with our friends. I might complain about having to write three essays every week compared to the two a term some of my friends at other universities are required to submit, but on a sunny summer's day nowhere can beat Oxford and it seems worth all the extra work it took both to get here and to stay here.

I've always been very goal-driven and competitive in every aspect of my life. As a kid I always wanted to get to the top of the stairs before my sister, be on every sports team regardless of whether I was actually any good or even liked the sport and get the highest grade in my prep. One of my biggest faults is that I always want to do everything at the same time and I won't take no for an answer. Coupling that with a really short attention span is a recipe for disaster when you're supposed to be focusing on getting a degree. At university I was Vice-Chair of the Commemoration Ball Committee and was trusted with £250,000 to give 1800 people the night of their lives. It was a great opportunity and the night was a huge success. Looking back at photographs of the way we transformed one quad into a fifties dance hall with a starlit sky and the deer park into a fairground I can't believe that I had a hand in creating something so spectacular. My role allowed me to be involved in a lot of the details as well as overseeing the big picture, which I loved as it meant I got to spend time with nearly all the members of the committee and meet lots of new people.

The year before I broke my back I was trying to get two more lacrosse Blues, be President of the Atalanta's Society (a members' club in Oxford at which Blues girls can get to know other Blues from different sports), pass the second-year part of my finals, run the most successful club nights in the city, be Vice-Chair of the Commemoration Ball Committee and date an Abercrombie model. Looking back I don't know how it all fitted in, but I'm grateful to have had the opportunity to experience all the best bits of uni life. Every night I went to parties (sometimes two or three with different themes – wardrobe nightmare!), drank champagne, got free entry everywhere and met new people. I'm not complaining of course – it was tons of fun but a pretty full-on occupation! My best memories are from nights out with my friends, punting and picnics with school friends or trips to Cambridge or University of East Anglia for lacrosse matches. Jodie and I would sometimes dress up and go out totally sober when we were in the middle of essays and had writer's block – nothing gives inspiration like dancing to cheesy dance music! We made a pact when I was in rehab at Stoke that even if we were seventy by the time stem cell research found a way to get me up on my legs again, Jodie and I would go to the Bridge nightclub in Oxford and dance all night . . . we'll see.

My time at Oxford wasn't how most people would expect Oxbridge life to be. Of course I worked hard and as I was studying joint subjects I would have two psychology essays and one physiology essay a week on top of statistics problems and lab reports. Once I'd learned to write essays in any situation and mastered the concept of the all-nighter I still had plenty of time around studying to play sport and go out. Jodie and I were 'Entz Reps' on the junior common room committee during my second year so we were allowed to choose the themes for the bi weekly bops. These ranged from bin bags (from which I made a pretty chic black and white prom dress) to nineties (I went as Tinkerbell as I'd just bought wings at Disneyland – I watched her in the nineties at least!) to 'P' bop (where Jodie and I went as pole dancers with our friend George as the pole). A bop is really just a school disco with alcohol held in the college bar but they always ended up being great nights. At the other end of the scale Lena and I were regulars in the Bridge VIP room when we weren't working at Filth. We both like to shop for dresses especially, so going out was the perfect showcase for our latest gorgeous purchases!

Basically, I think breaking my back was a good thing to happen to me, both from a life-plan point of view to keep me off the standard 'Oxford degree–banker/management consultant in the City–marry Oxbridge man' path and from a personality point of view as I was becoming more and more uncompromising and my priorities were totally skewed. Had I continued the way I was going through my final year of university I probably would have failed my course, lost my school friends and my close relationship with my family, and got sick from exhaustion. Ending up in a chair changed everything: many of my university friends ditched me as I was too shy in the chair to go out dancing, unless I was with Lena and we had our table at the club, because everyone knew me and stared or asked questions; and I couldn't get into other people's rooms for pre-drinks and, aside from Jodie, nobody thought to relocate to my room. Jodie did organize a big drinks party at the end of my first term back but it was painfully awkward as most of the rest of the guests had been ignoring me for eight weeks.

When I first went back to Oxford four days after leaving Stoke Mandeville I focused on studying but after doing all twenty-four essays for the term in the first two weeks and getting my two dissertations in before term even started that didn't work. I also hated going to lectures as I had to sit in weird spots – thankfully Guy and Lena always sat with me even if they were on the floor. Gradually my sporty friends persuaded me to stay involved with that side of my life too and my first big night out was with the Atalanta's girls for the annual Vinnie's/Atalanta's dinner. I was president of the society still so Ellaine, the ex-president and a close friend, was determined to get me up the stairs at Vinnie's. My friends George and Dan carried me up the two sets of stairs and at the end of the night we found the least drunk rugby Blue to carry me back down. It ended up being a great night and showed me that being in a chair didn't mean I had to become a hermit. After my accident the Bridge became too much of a hassle as it was up two flights of stairs so we relocated to the conveniently ground-floor-located Kukui and the bar at the Randolph, where they ended up naming a cocktail after Lena!

Getting onto GB Rowing and the British Paralympic Association fast-track athletics programme was a complete life-saver for me as I was really struggling with the psychological side of being disabled. Once I started going out again I felt even more as if people were looking at me and talking about my situation, which they probably were. I pretended it didn't bother me, though. Wheelchair users are few and far between at Oxford and having been on the door at so many club nights before my injury there were a lot of people who recognized me and wondered what had happened. Thanks to those outlets I could focus on sport to prove to people that I wasn't just a disabled person to feel sorry for – I could still kick their asses in a fitness test and I wanted to be in the Paralympics one day. Funnily enough, the more media attention I got when I took up sport, the more the old crowd seemed to want to be friends again but I was happy to turn down every invitation! I'm secure enough in the friendships I've kept and those that I've made to make my own decisions and work towards the things that I really want now, rather than what I think I should want.

6

School: Preparing Me for Life

At school, as part of my A2-level PE course, I had to devise and carry out a personal exercise plan (PEP). Along with my best friend Izzie I worked out in the gym or on the cross-country course twice a day for eight weeks during Lent term in our final year. At the end of the eight weeks we planned to have developed abs defined enough that we could train in crop tops. And of course improve our test scores for aerobic fitness, flexibility and strength. Ironically, still now one of my biggest motivators when I really want to eat that piece of cake or feel too tired to go to the gym is that I want to keep my flat stomach so I can still fit into all my clothes from my athletics days!

We'd set ourselves what I thought at the time was an extremely hard programme, on top of which I had to train as part of the school lacrosse team and continue to take tennis lessons, so I was convinced we must be training more than anybody. On a typical day we would go to the gym in one of our morning free periods and do twenty minutes on the cross-trainer and then some core stability exercises. Then at lunchtime we would have lacrosse practice that led directly into a classroom PE class so afterwards we would stay in the sports centre and do another gym workout focusing on core stability and toning muscle. I was exhausted coupling this with taking four A2 levels but looking back at the graphs I drew of the results of our training I'm quite impressed by the amount of improvement in fitness that this in reality not very intense training programme brought about. In twelve weeks my VO2 max increased by 11.9 ml/kg/min. This means that my body could take in and use 11.9 ml more oxygen per minute for each kilogram I weighed which is a significant rise for less than three months of training. In fact, according to the standard guidelines for the bleep test that we used to measure our fitness, my cardiovascular fitness level was 'superior' for my age and sex. Based on this, if an elite junior athlete took the test we used they would certainly go off the scale. My VO2 max has not been measured since I left the GB Rowing programme so I'd be interested to see how it has changed since the days of my A-level PE training programme.

I was incredibly lucky to have had the opportunity to attend the number-one ranked secondary school in Britain, Wycombe Abbey, from the age of thirteen. Until then I had been at a small all-girls school in Gerrards Cross in Buckinghamshire called St Mary's where I was bullied horribly for being overweight and quite socially awkward. At ballet class when I was in junior school we were asked who our favourite singer was and as Mum likes to bring up when I'm talking about music, which now I love, I told the teacher I was a fan of Leonard Cohen and Lionel Ritchie as they were Mum's favourites. I had no idea who Backstreet Boys or Boyzone, cited by my classmates, were! And despite being sports obsessed and my mother watching my diet like a hawk, I couldn't seem to shift my baby fat. As a kid, grapes were my version of sweets and until my sister was born when I was six, after which Mum had less time to look out for my diet, I didn't eat crisps or chocolate, or drink fizzy drinks. The one exception was once a week at the sports club: after Dad had played his hockey match my best friend Kat and I would be allowed to sit on the high bar stools with a ginger beer and a packet of crisps. We felt so grown up! Being less than popular at junior school wasn't all bad, though. The friends I did have were great and I can still remember going bowling or to the Crystal Maze adventure attraction with my few close friends for my birthday parties. I also worked hard and got good grades, winning the 'achievement' prize at the school speech day five years in a row, which made my parents very proud. My parents both place very high value on working hard and achieving your goals so it didn't take long for me to work out that the more I achieved in school, the more trips to Thorpe Park we went on!

During year seven I went to Wycombe Abbey for an away tennis match and was blown away by the incredible facilities at this Hogwarts-esque Eden in the middle of dingy High Wycombe. I couldn't believe how vast the grounds were or how self-assured and grown-up all the girls looked. I was desperate to be one of them. As always I didn't sit around with an empty dream – I wanted to make it a reality. Mum still shakes her head when she recounts how I requested a Wycombe Abbey prospectus online and approached her and Dad about getting a place there. The fees were far too high and my parents didn't want me to board, so in order to have a chance of moving to such an amazing school for year nine I would have to get a major scholarship. Wycombe Abbey is predominantly a boarding school so at the late stage I was applying I'd also need to be a scholar to be considered for a day place.

Wycombe Abbey 13+ scholarship exams make Oxford University finals look a doddle when you consider that they are taken by twelve-year-old children. As well as exams in all the usual maths/science/English areas you had to take papers in two different languages. I opted for French and German as my Latin and Italian were too basic for the level required. I needed to be able to read and interpret a newspaper article in the foreign language. I can't begin to count how many practice articles I analysed with the help of Mum's French skills for that paper as I was sure the language scholarship was the only one I had a hope of getting. Once the written papers were over you then had to have an unscripted conversation in one foreign language (in my case French) with a Wycombe Abbey teacher before your interview (in English thankfully!) with the headmistress, an incredible lady called Mrs Davies. She had an amazing talent for remembering everyone's name and a few facts about them so she would always be able to ask relevant questions about your life when you came back after a weekend exeat. By the end of the intense two days I spent at the school I was sure I'd blown my chances of ever going there again. When the letter came a few weeks later announcing that I'd been awarded the William Johnston Yapp Science Scholarship I couldn't have been happier or more amazed. Not only did I get to leave St Mary's and start afresh at a place where I wasn't just regarded as being a fat kid, I would be among people who were way cleverer than I was and therefore hopefully not bullied for my grades anymore. Oh, and my new school looked like a fairy-tale castle complete with lake and forest!

Wycombe Abbey lived up to all my high expectations. I absolutely loved every minute I spent there and I really hope that one day I'll be able to send my children to such an amazing school. I lost the last of my puppy fat during the holidays before I started at Wycombe Abbey as I spent it working at the stables in order to earn free riding lessons or hacks on the riding-school ponies. It was hard work but it taught me to have a good work ethic and instilled the idea that anything worth having is worth working for. This rapid weight loss unexpectedly left all my mufti far too big for me so on my first weekend of school Mum took me shopping and I could finally fit into the fashionable clothes everyone else had. Unfortunately at that time the fashion revolved around baggy neon cargo pants with strips of fabric dangling off them and cropped vests with zippers all over them from Punky Fish. Combine that with the thick fringe I was struggling to grow out and it was not a pretty sight but I finally felt like I fitted in somewhere.

The one downside to my change in schools was that Wycombe Abbey is very much a lacrosse school. I played school and club hockey, and had no idea what a lacrosse stick even looked like. Although I was one of forty girls starting in the upper fourth that year, most of my fellow new girls came from feeder schools such as Godstowe and so had been playing pop lacrosse practically since they could walk. There was a fun hockey group that met once a week, though, so I joined that but it didn't take long for me to catch the lacrosse bug. In addition to PE lessons nearly every day, students up to the fifth form had stick work lessons on Saturday mornings where they improved their lacrosse skills. Or in my case learned some.

I tried really hard in all our lacrosse lessons and was selected as goalkeeper for the U14B team in my first term. I was so proud but looking back I'm pretty sure it wasn't thanks to me having any skill; it was more just because I turned up to every practice and was evidently as desperate to be in the team as they were to find someone who didn't mind standing in goal with balls being hurled at their head. Nevertheless, I got my wish and continued to play for the school teams in goal all the way up the ladder until I was goalkeeper for the school 2nd XII. Although I was happy to play for the team in any capacity I was never thrilled to be made goalkeeper as I love to run and although you do move around a fair bit in goal it's not quite the same as playing out on the field. I was made stick-work captain and lacrosse captain for my house, Rubens House, in the lower sixth so I did get to play on the field in house matches at least!

With school-team practices before school once a week, at two lunchtimes and after school on a Friday, plus house practices and matches twice a week and hockey practice another lunchtime, I seemed to spend a lot of time on a sports pitch while I was at Wycombe Abbey. It wasn't all play and no work though – after all, that's not how a school reaches the top of the *Sunday Times* schools guide list repeatedly! All the staff at Wycombe Abbey are incredibly smart people who must be the best teachers in their field as it never felt like we were working unusually hard yet when it came to exams they had miraculously managed to get most of the facts into our heads. I remember in particular cramming for GCSEs with Rose and realizing that neither of us had actually finished reading *Pride and Prejudice* – we had just studied the sections we went over in class and left it at that. Thank goodness for the Colin Firth-starring BBC TV adaptation! We watched it start to finish one exeat at Rose's house in Hastings and came back with a vague knowledge of the story. When the exam came I just answered on the sections Mrs Day had taught us and came out with a high A*. All without having finished the text. We were so well drilled in the mark schemes for the other subjects that by the time the Geography mock GCSE exams came round the points in my long answers read in almost the same order as the mark scheme!

The one thing I hated was that I was a day girl, as I felt like I missed out on the best bits of school. I was usually there for breakfast as dropping me off early avoided Dad getting stuck in the rush-hour traffic. With sports practices and after-school lectures combined with Wycombe Abbey days running until 5.25 p.m. I was not at home very much, so I asked my housemistress if they could find a bed for me. I had to wait a year as our house was full but in the sixth form I got my wish and became a boarder and never had to leave. With the Wycombe Abbey schedule of lacrosse practices from 7 a.m. and lectures finishing at 9 p.m. I think it was a relief to my parents too that they didn't have to spend their lives running a taxi service!

It's not surprising really that most of my closest friends are still the ones I made at school. Rose, in particular, has seen me through ten years of adjustments, having been my mentor when I first started at Wycombe Abbey as a chavvy thirteen-year-old among sophisticated boarding-school girls. We were both in Rubens House and then opted to be in the same flat in Clarence, the upper-sixth campus-style house. Clarence brought about a whole new era of fun. That was when my core group of Rose, Izzie, Ceci and Lou formed. Izzie and I were both taking science and PE A levels – she is now a doctor and at that time I thought I wanted to be a vet – so we spent every lesson together. We must have been a total nightmare for our science teachers. Biology in particular we found fairly straightforward so the lessons were largely extended battles in the highlighter war. In chemistry class Rose, Izzie and I managed to set fire to a desk with a Bunsen burner, which was only a minor glitch until I threw the ubiquitous science-lab blue paper towels on it to put it out. Unsurprisingly, they went up in flames too!

Through Izzie I met Ceci as we were in the same group for the Duke of Edinburgh's Gold Award practice expedition to Dartmoor. The summer we went, Dartmoor was hit by the worst storms in sixty years and one night they actually had to put all our tents in a marquee to stop them blowing away. It wasn't the best introduction to the Gold Award but the experience certainly brought us closer! It also taught us that the best way to avoid being tasked with navigation for the assessed expedition in Snowdonia the following Easter (vital when none of you can read a compass) was to throw our maps off the first quarry we came to. By the time we'd finished the Award we were pretty close friends so when Ceci, Izzie, Rose and I were all put in the same flat for one term in Clarence we knew it was going to be a good one. Ceci's best friend Lou was also housed with us, and when we split up to go to university, Lou and I grew even closer as we both opted to go to Oxford.

Clarence House is run more like a university than a school, with the upper sixth cooking their own breakfast and dinner and living in halls-style accommodation. We were also allowed out on Wednesday and Friday nights into Wycombe to go to McDonald's, which was a much-awaited burst of freedom. It's amazing the state we managed to get into at McDonald's. To get back from the town to school we had to cross a series of mini-roundabouts around a central grassy area. One Friday we'd obviously had a few too many milkshakes and our friend Anna slipped while climbing over the wall into this area and sprained her ankle. It took two of the girls nearly twenty minutes to get her back from there to where Clarence was situated on the hill so we went ahead and explained the situation in what I thought was a very sober and convincing way. It wasn't until I went back to give a talk to the sixth-form students three years after my accident that Mrs Tear introduced me by bringing up this incident as an example of how Izzie and I weren't exactly the best-behaved students in our year! She had a point, though. We managed to break into the disused RAF base the other side of the school woods when we were just 'going for a walk', just happening to remove a fence post, crawl through the gap and 'accidentally' climb into the base. We then had to walk all the way through the base to find an exit onto the main road so we could get back into school for tea. At bed check another night, Mrs Tear checked Lou's room and she wasn't there. We all tried to explain where she might be while standing in the corridor outside her room. She and Izzie calmly opened the door a few minutes later and nearly knocked her over as they had just climbed in through the window. I don't know how we thought all this passed the teachers by!

After such a great five years at Wycombe Abbey, and particularly after the fun we had in Clarence, I was very sad when it was our turn to graduate. My eighteenth birthday had been during our A2s so on the day of graduation I threw a big party at home with an inflatable obstacle course, a duelling game, traditional fairground stalls and a big barbecue. The weather was awful and I cried and cried to my then boyfriend Olly that nobody was going to turn up and it would be a terrible day. I'd never thrown a big birthday party before and was terrified it would flop. As it happens it was such a huge success that it lasted over twelve hours. In the evening everyone who was left congregated in the big lounge upstairs in the barn and my musical friends sang and played guitar and piano. Looking back it sounds horribly cheesy but in reality it was the perfect way to end my school days.

7

Getting into Paralympic Sport

Ordinarily a 5000 m race, twelve and a half laps of the track, would be the last thing I would watch but it's lunchtime at Stoke Mandeville NSIC so I have an hour to kill. May as well spend it watching the Beijing Paralympics. Even when the athletes are stationary on the start line, I feel myself getting interested. The girls look so strong and lean and, although they are all in wheelchairs, they are a world away from the massive, heavy contraptions the hospital has lent me. The back wheels are cambered and most of them use carbon disc wheels like elite track cyclists. Between these the girls seem to be kneeling over a long tube that goes down to a smaller front wheel and has some sort of steering mechanism attached. Looking at them lined up on the start, you can tell that these are real athletes and their disability, although it should be brought to the surface by the fact that they are competing in wheelchairs, is the last thing you notice.

From the moment the gun goes to start the women's 5000 m T54 final, it is obvious that the race is going to be tactical, with the girls quickly slotting into a group and playing each other off to try to avoid pulling the pack. I'm pretty surprised at how much the set-up looks like the peloton in the Tour de France, only with fewer people. The front wheels of the girls behind seem to be slotted between the back wheels of those in front and the girls push hard and then brake for a moment to stay right in the slipstream without hitting the back of the chair in front. Along the straights the pack fans out across the lanes as girls try to get themselves out of boxed-in positions or get a lead on other athletes. Then around the bends it is like they have been sucked into a tunnel as everyone jostles for the ideal position close to the inside lane but not so far inside that they would be boxed in by slower athletes on their outside.

Coming off the bend onto the home straight of the penultimate lap after nearly eleven minutes of racing there's a pack of six girls led by two Swiss athletes, in their distinctive red lycra with the white cross on the back, followed closely by another pack of four athletes. I can't believe the speed they're going after eleven hard laps of the track. They've suddenly upped the tempo and now nobody's missing pushes to stay behind in the draught; everyone seems to be pushing flat out so gaps are starting to open out. Then all of a sudden the Swiss girl on the right flips over and takes out half of the pack. Only four girls manage to avoid the carnage and they continue to zoom around for the final lap. Then as they approach the mess of chairs and bodies where the crash occurred, to go past for the final sprint down the home straight, a pair of Chinese officials suddenly run across the track in front of them. The American girl has to brake to avoid them and the British girl has to swerve outside so their sprint finish becomes more of a slalom. I can't believe how unprofessional the officials were – that would never have happened in an Olympic final! In the end only five girls cross the finish line in what is definitely the most exciting athletics event I've seen. In the end they had to re run the final due to the interference of the officials but this race was brilliant viewing even if it couldn't be counted as an official race.

Before I broke my back I only vaguely knew of two people with a disability, friends of my mother who both became paralysed after falling off horses. To be honest I never considered either of these ladies to be disabled as they were powerhouses who got on with life as though their spinal injuries were minor blips in their life plan. I remember soon after I had my accident one of them telling my mother that I just had to get on with it, which was a pretty unique take on the situation given that all Mum's other friends were offering sympathy and support, but I think it helped her as much as any of the well-wishing. My general perception of a disabled person was someone who needed care and was unable to live a normal life. It was someone to feel sorry for. I remember discussing a friend of a friend who had had a spinal injury while I was staying with Rose the weekend before I broke my back and I was firmly of the opinion that I would rather die than spend the rest of my life in a wheel-chair – until then I was never superstitious about tempting fate but the timing is fairly ironic! Although I now know that being in a wheelchair really isn't such a bad thing I wouldn't wish the patronizing behaviour I receive on any of my friends.

Even after I moved to Stoke Mandeville and was surrounded by other patients with spinal injuries I didn't really see myself as one of them. I would never push around the hospital in shorts with surgical stockings and a catheter bag on display to the world. There are some things you have to endure when you're first injured but they don't need to be shared with everyone who visits the hospital. Even now when I work out at the gym in Stoke Mandeville Stadium next to the spinal unit, I see wheelchair users sporting this rather strange and frankly inappropriate look and I question why being in a wheelchair makes some people lose the will to fit into normal society. Maybe it's me who has the wrong idea, though. I take care to try to look like an able-bodied person who happens to sit in a wheelchair whereas some wheelchair users are happy to accept their disability and allow themselves to fit into the stereotype people like the pre-accident me have of a 'disabled person'.

My unwillingness to allow my disability to dominate who I am carried through to my initial choice of sports. My first experience of Paralympic sport came while still in rehab at Stoke Mandeville. During my stay at the NSIC I tried many wheelchair sports, from tennis to hockey to basketball, and although I enjoyed them I saw them as inferior adaptations of their Olympic counterparts. That changed when the Beijing Paralympics started. I'd never paid much attention to the Paralympics – in fact I'm not even sure I knew they were taking place after the Olympics in 2008 – but being in hospital adapting to life in a wheelchair seemed like a pretty good time to start taking an interest.

I found the contact details online for all the sports that caught my eye in the Beijing coverage and emailed the federations with a bit of background about my previous sporting ability and current situation. The rowing, athletics, swimming, skiing and cycling federations all got back to me almost immediately, which was a great surprise as I expected everyone to be out at the Paralympic Games, not bothering to email me! Of these, rowing and athletics appealed the most as I had rowed before my accident and the track racing was what had initially drawn me into watching the Paralympics.

While I was still in the spinal unit I met with Ian Thompson, then Chairman of the British Wheelchair Racing Association, and his wife Baroness Tanni Grey-Thompson during a Paralympic handover event from Beijing to London that was held at Stoke Mandeville Stadium. Ian helped me into a chair for the first time and showed me how to push around the track with a strange pair of gloves made from tape that held your hands in the correct position for pushing a racing chair. Unlike pushing an everyday chair, in the racing chairs we have a push rim set inside the wheel and the power to move forward is generated by pushing with your fist inside this rim so the friction moves the push rim and in turn the wheel. This was a very alien concept to me and I kept trying to grip the rim like I would on my normal wheelchair. After only a lap I was exhausted! Thankfully Ian seemed to think I had potential and lent me his old racing chair, which was a top-of-the-range Top End kneeling frame exactly like the one

I push in now. The downside of this was that I struggled to transfer into it, being so newly injured with a lot of residual muscle bulk in my legs and very poor balance, and this and the stares I received pushing around in a long wheelchair at very slow speed when I got back to university put me off the sport after only a couple of tries.

I didn't like doing a sport that was so obviously disabled because it involved a wheelchair, so I decided to focus on rowing. Tom Dyson, the Head Coach of the Great Britain adaptive rowing programme, invited me to go to Caversham where the team are based and be fitted for a rowing seat. I was so nervous when Mum picked me up from the hospital for our appointment – I wasn't even sure if I'd be able to transfer on and off the seat let alone actually row in this new way! Thankfully Tom was very patient and the fitting went without a hitch. One of the massive benefits for me with rowing was that I could train on the ergo in the gym at Stoke Mandeville. When I went back to Oxford after leaving hospital I took the ergo I had at home and put it in my room, allowing me to train in private without the hassle of getting across town to a track or a gym. A month after I left Stoke Mandeville the National Indoor Rowing Championships took place and I was invited to race. We had to row 1 km on a static ergo and I finished in last place, over a minute behind Helene Raynsford, who won the gold medal in the arms-only class in Beijing (the class I was part of). Surprisingly though, given my competitive nature, I was actually really pleased with my performance and enjoyed the event a lot – our race was integrated into the able-bodied programme, too, so we even started with the junior able-bodied boys who had to row the same distance.

I was incredibly lucky during the six months that I trained for adaptive rowing to have the help and support of the GB programme. Tom devised training programmes tailored to building my strength and fitness and I was invited to two GB Rowing winter training camps. In reality I wasn't ready for the rigorous training of a week-long winter camp where we would train three times per day, doing a mixture of strength and conditioning, ergo rowing sessions and steady-state handbiking, but I gave it my best shot. Despite having played a lot of sport and trained regularly at school and university, I had never experienced the pain of an elite training session and how much you ache all the time between but still have to get back on the ergo or the bike for the next session. The blisters I developed on my ribcage from the strap holding me onto the seat have left scars that still show up when I'm tanned! By the second camp it was obvious that I wasn't improving at a fast enough rate to keep my place on the GB development squad and Tom gently suggested I train independently for a while and come back for re trials later in the year. I was absolutely gutted.

The GB adaptive rowing programme is very compact in terms of the number of athletes and over the course of the winter I'd become very close to Helene, with whom Tom had put me in a room. I was so shy towards her at first as she was one of the best Paralympic athletes in Britain, with a Paralympic gold medal and multiple world championship titles, but she soon made me feel at ease. She shares my interest in neuroscience so it was really nice to be able to geek out a bit and have someone really intelligent with whom to discuss the dissertation I was working on – I didn't get that luxury with the track athletes! As Tom had hoped, Helene was brilliant at helping me get into the mindset of being an elite athlete, but even she struggled to teach me to look after my body and know when a niggle or sniffle meant I could train and when it was a signal that I needed to take a session off. I was so desperate to improve that I would train even if I'd woken up with a heart rate over 100 beats per minute (when healthy my heart rate sits around 50 bpm and anything over 55 is a signal that I could be overtraining or coming down with something). This led to me getting ill and injured, and therefore not improving, so eventually I was dropped from the squad.

In addition to Helene teaching me how to behave like an elite athlete I also picked up more tips on being in a wheelchair from her during the two weeks we roomed together than I had during my entire time in rehab. The physiotherapists at Stoke Mandeville were fantastic at teaching me the textbook way to do everything, but as none of them are wheelchair users they would have no way of knowing that the textbook methods can actually make things harder. For example, I was taught in rehab that before transferring I should put the brakes on my chair beside what I want to sit on and transfer sideways. In reality transferring is a lot easier when you don't use your brakes as then you can move the wheelchair as you push up to get a better angle for your shoulders to push through. It's also a lot quicker and makes you look a lot less crippled if people don't have to wait twenty minutes while you line up chairs and fiddle with brakes!

Helene did a lot of Pilates when she was rowing and although initially I was a little sceptical about how someone with no leg movement and very little trunk control like myself would be able to do the movements, it does actually work. Pilates is a great way to stretch and wash away the residual adrenaline that can keep you pumped for hours after finishing cardiovascular training. It also helps to prevent injury as a lot of the movements focus on using the smaller stabilizing muscles around your joints, so there is a far lower chance of them becoming damaged when the larger muscles are working hard in either rowing or wheelchair athletics. It can be difficult to join in able-bodied classes at the gym as they tend to do a lot of the movements standing up but I still use the Pilates exercises I learned from the strength coaches at GB Rowing as part of my weekly workout routine. Because I haven't been in a chair very long my shoulders and arms are still not entirely used to being used as legs so I do get niggles and minor tears fairly frequently. By working my rotator cuff muscles and stretching every day I hope I can keep these to a minimum.

I also stand every day when I'm at home in a special wooden frame that supports my ankles, knees and hips in order to stretch out my hip flexors and try to keep the bone density in my legs at a healthy level. It's very common for wheelchair users to break bones in the limbs they don't use as the lack of weight-bearing causes the bones to become very brittle just like in osteoporosis. It is also common for wheelchair users to become so tight through their hip flexors that they can't lie on their front without arching their back as a result of sitting down most of the time. I'm determined to try to keep my body as close to the way it was before my accident in terms of posture as it seems to me that if people were built to be standing up, then even though I now sit down, the most natural position for my legs to be in would be the standing position. It doesn't make sense therefore to let my muscles and tendons change length to the extent that they won't allow me to be in the position my body was built for. Saying that, it is still a struggle to maintain the flexibility in my hip joint and prevent them from calcifying into the sitting position. Having the opportunity to walk in Ekso Bionics' incredible exo skeleton has been a great incentive to keep up all the stretching though! It's an awesome piece of technology involving a sort of cage that fits around my legs and straps around my torso and has articulated joints in the same place as my own. An in-built computer then controls the device so when I move a hip forward and to one side it cues a series of movements in that leg of the exo skeleton causing my leg to move as though I'm walking. Put this into a series with me moving my hips slightly from side to side every time I want to make a step and I'm walking! I could never afford to buy this device but I love getting the chance to demonstrate it at exhibitions sometimes as it means I get to feel what it's like to walk again. That's what sets the Ekso Bionics device apart from other similar machines – because the limbs are articulated and it takes all of its own weight it truly does feel to me like walking did (aside from needing to use crutches with it as I'm not too steady on my feet!). Physically this is obviously awesome, but the main benefit for me is mental. I feel so much more confident presenting to thousands of people standing up in the Ekso suit than I do sitting down, and when I'm talking to people one-on-one wearing the suit I can look them in the eye which honestly changes the way people talk to me. With my job and having been an athlete I'm very used to presenting from my chair now so I hadn't even realized how at a disadvantage sitting down when I present made me, but now I've had the opportunity to present standing up a few times in Ekso I wish I could use it every time I'm presenting.

By some stroke of luck the timing of losing my support from GB Rowing worked out perfectly. I had been on the British Paralympic Association's Fast Track Power and Performance athletics programme for throwing alongside my rowing training through the winter, having been 'spotted' at a Paralympic talent day in London. This really only consisted of going to Loughborough once a month for a weekend on top of the rowing training I was already doing, so I could balance the two fairly easily. It also gave me the chance to learn from some amazing Paralympians, such as John McFall, the T42 runner, and Nathan Stephens, the F57 javelin thrower. This was the first time I'd really met people with disabilities other than wheelchair users and

I'll admit I was pretty jealous of the blade runners with their cool carbon fibre legs. John in particular always wore shorts and spurned the usual leg design, where it is covered in fabric that is supposed to resemble skin, going for just having the bare mechanics. Very Terminator-esque!

I quickly became friends with the rest of the squad, in particular with Scott Moorhouse, a javelin thrower who very soon after we started on the programme became ranked in the top three in the world. He drove a tiny red convertible sports car that I was desperate to have a go in so, as we lived really close to each other, for one of the camps he drove me up to Loughborough. My car hadn't arrived yet when the camps started so it saved Mum a trip up the motorway! Getting my chair in the car was a bit of a palaver but, unlike some of my able-bodied friends who had said flat out that my chair wouldn't fit in their much bigger cars, to Scott it was just another piece of equipment that would be fitted in somehow. That really sums up the effect going to the Fast Track Power and Performance camps had on my perception of my own disability. I stopped thinking of my wheelchair as some really important part of my life and it became a matter-of-fact mode of transport to get into when I needed to move like an able-bodied person. The amputees were so comfortable with taking off their prosthetic limbs and showing off their stumps that I realized I didn't need to be sensitive about my disability either.

When my beautiful new Mini Clubman finally did arrive the first long drive I did was to Loughborough for a Fast

Track Power and Performance camp. I was such a wreck when I arrived that I didn't do any training that morning. Being on the main roads with cars zooming past reminded me far too much of the drive leading up to my accident and I was terrified it would repeat itself. I was nervous for months whenever I drove long distances. Most people thought I was crazy wanting to get a Mini but I was completely determined not to go for any other car. We looked at Volkswagens first but I wasn't remotely interested in them, and once I'd started looking at the cars in the Mini garage Mum had to ring and cancel our next appointment as even the prospect of an A-Class Merc couldn't distract me from my Mini fetish. I tried the smaller cars but getting my chair in and out would have been a bit of a hassle at that point. Then they showed me the Clubman and it was like the car had been designed for wheelchair users. The boot doors open outwards rather than upwards so it's way easier for me to get things into the boot without having to duck under it. It even has a little door behind the driver's seat so I can put my dirty wheels in behind me without having to pass them over my body and get all muddy. I'd found my dream car! As I have very little trunk control I had to get sports seats to stop me sliding off when going around roundabouts, and of course I had to have hand controls to allow me to drive. The controls are remarkably simple to use, thankfully. I wasn't required to take any sort of test before being allowed out on the roads with them so it's a good job I only had to remember 'push' to stop and 'pull' to go! Through the Motability scheme I ordered a beautiful British racing-green Mini Clubman, called Mabel, on a three-year lease and after three years of begging my parents for a Mini, which they quite rightly refused, I joined my friends in the Mini owners' club! Sytner High Wycombe, where we bought Mabel, now sponsor me, so when the lease ran out on her they gave me a gorgeous light-blue Clubman called Millie. I clock up a lot of miles driving up north for training and races, and for work events, so I spend a lot of time in Millie – she's absolutely perfect. I can fit my racing chair into the car easily just by putting the back seats down and she's low enough that I can even reach to put extra equipment on the roof rack when there are two of us travelling anywhere. When I'm tired I also love that the seat is pretty much level with my everyday chair, which means I'm a lot less likely to miss the transfer and land on the floor if I have jelly arms after a marathon!

The weekend before I lost my place on the rowing programme I had attended the final Fast Track Power and Performance camp, and Tanni was the guest speaker. By this time I'd returned Ian's chair to him but we'd stayed in contact and I was interested in giving track athletics another try, so he came up to Loughborough with a couple of racing chairs as well. This time he'd brought a chair with a footplate for me to use which I could get in easily; that made me feel a lot more positive about the sport from the start as I didn't have to ask for assistance before training even began. After a rocky start, in which I flipped the chair over backwards trying to set the steering in a straight line on the indoor track, we went out and pushed for three hours around the university campus. My rowing training had improved my fitness and strength enough that I was able to focus on the technique of pushing the chair rather than getting exhausted over a short distance. I loved the adrenaline rush of going down hills so much that I happily climbed to the top of the hill over and over again to try to improve my downhill speed – helpfully shown on the speed warning display at the side of the road. My best was 15 mph. To put that into context I hit 46.1 mph during the Tyne Tunnel 2K race in 2011 and push faster than 15 mph on the flat when I track race, so it wasn't exactly world-beating stuff but it felt incredible!

I started racing as a bit of a joke really. Ian suggested I come to the Silverstone Half Marathon, one week after that first (and only) training session, to watch the race. It was the day after rowing had waved me off and I was in a bit of a state, which I think probably played a part in Ian deciding to distract me by allowing me to take part in the half marathon. To my surprise I managed to complete the distance and achieved the qualifying time for the 2009 London Marathon. As well as it being a great experience to race on the Silverstone circuit alongside so many runners, I really enjoyed meeting the athletes before and after the race. The atmosphere in the pit garage assigned to the wheelchair athletes was totally different to that of rowing. There were so many more athletes and coaches split into their training groups. Ian and Tanni were coaching Paralympian Brian Alldis who was really friendly and gave me lots of tips about which parts of the course to watch out for and when I should save my energy.

The general vibe at Silverstone was far more relaxed than I'd got used to with rowing, with lots of older ex-Paralympians taking part for fun alongside Paralympic medallists from Beijing like Mickey Bushell. I quickly got caught up in their excitement over the season starting again and couldn't wait to enter all the road and track meets coming up that everyone was talking about. That atmosphere at Silverstone and a few weeks later at Redcar Half Marathon is what keeps me road racing whenever I can fit it in, even though I no longer see them as races and more as a training session with empty roads.

8

Spinal Games and London Marathon 2009

As well as being a pioneering figure in terms of the treatment of spinal cord injury in Europe, Sir Ludwig Guttmann is seen as the 'father' of the Paralympic movement. In 1948, while London was hosting the Olympic Games, Guttmann decided to run a 'parallel' competition for the spinally injured Second World War veterans in his care as a way to encourage them to build up their strength and fitness as well as restore their competitive spirit ready for returning to everyday life – hence the origin of the name Paralympic Games. This became an annual event, and in 1952 spinally injured patients from the Netherlands were invited to join the Stoke Mandeville Games, turning it into an international event for the first time.

By 1960 the competition had grown, with athletes from five continents taking part, and for the first time the Games were held outside Stoke Mandeville, in Rome, directly following the Olympic Games that year. This was a major breakthrough for Guttmann, who aimed one day to have the competition integrated into the Olympic Games. Fittingly, London 2012 was the first time an Olympic and Paralympic Games have been organized by the same committee, bringing them one step closer to Guttmann's dream of equal competition for disabled athletes. Whether or not full integration will ever occur remains to be seen, as the International Olympic Committee and the International Paralympic Committee currently strive to maintain a degree of separation. The Rome 'Stoke Mandeville Games' also included athletes with other disabilities rather than solely spinal cord injuries, and so are often considered the first Paralympic Games, although this name was not adopted until 1984. By this time the International Paralympic Committee had been set up to govern this quadrennial sports event, but the Stoke Mandeville Games (now known as the Inter Spinal Unit Games, or 'Spinal Games') continue to run annually at Stoke Mandeville. Now though they are solely for patients who have been spinally injured for less than a year to get a chance to experience competitive disability sport and socialize with people from other hospitals in the UK and Europe who have been through similar experiences.

My experience of competing at the Inter Spinal Unit Games in 2009 was slightly different to that of most of my team-mates and competitors. I was thrilled to be selected as the only girl on the eight-strong team representing the Stoke Mandeville NSIC. I had to compete in archery, table tennis, shooting and swimming (bowls being the fifth sport contested, which thankfully I didn't have to do!). The sports are chosen so that even very newly injured people with high-level injuries are able to take part in the paraplegic or quadriplegic divisions. At the time of selection towards the end of 2008 I was training in adaptive rowing so spending a week at the Spinal Games at the end of April 2009 wasn't a big problem. However, by the time the Games came around I'd swapped to athletics and was set to complete my first London Marathon the day after the competition ended. Not great timing! Thankfully Ian, my coach, was running track-taster sessions at the Spinal Games, so we used these as an opportunity for me to train for the marathon between my events.

For most of the competitors the Spinal Games are their first experience of competing in disabled sport, and for many it is the first time they've stayed in an unfamiliar environment since they became spinally injured. In fact for some it's their first trip out of hospital. When I think back to the first time I spent a night away from the safe and familiar surroundings of the hospital I'm quite envious of the people for whom the Spinal Games acts as a stepping stone between hospital and a normal trip away: having other wheelchair users and indeed physios and other helping hands around would definitely have eased the shock of being back in the real world for any amount of time after a long period in the bubble of the spinal unit. The competitors from Glasgow fly down to the Spinal Games and I have to say I'm also quite jealous that their first plane ride in a wheelchair is with a support team of hospital staff and friends from their spinal injuries unit. My first flight was to Lou's twenty-first on Jersey and it actually went very smoothly thanks to being surrounded by all my friends, who mothered me very effectively. On the way home, though, a particularly awful air steward started joking that I must have drunk way too much over the weekend to need a wheelchair. We tried to laugh it off but he wouldn't leave it, even to the extent that my friend Rose had to almost force him to bring the aisle chair to take me from my seat to the gate where my everyday chair was waiting. He still insisted I should just walk!

I'm really glad I was able to compete in the Spinal Games, and that I now have the opportunity to go back and coach athletics and cycling at them every year. Although at first I was apprehensive about sharing a dormitory with seven guys I hadn't seen in five months along with Selina, my rehab physiotherapist from my time in the NSIC, and Georgie, the Head of Sport, it took only minutes for us to bond over the endless supply of tea and biscuits and I've stayed in contact with most of the team. Among us were the ex-motocross rider, ex-oil rig worker and ex-army parachute jumper who were in rehab at the same time as me and co-developed the brilliant game of wheelchair hockey, and a quadriplegic who had also been in the unit with us, so it was great to get the chance to reminisce about our time there and catch up on what everyone had been up to for the past six months.

I've never made a point of trying to have friends in

wheelchairs – I don't think that being in a chair has changed me fundamentally as a person so I still feel just as close to my non-disabled friends as I did before. However, sometimes it's nice to be able to talk to someone who understands all the other parts of being in a wheelchair, aside from the obvious lack of leg use, that people who haven't experienced it don't see. Through athletics and rowing I do now have a lot of friends who are wheelchair users and they are all great people I would want to hang out with whether I was in a chair or not.

5 a.m.: My alarm goes off in my room in the London Marathon race hotel but I'm not sure why I bothered to set it, as I've been up most of the night contemplating whether I'm going to be sick with nerves now or when I get to the race. Possibly the course map wasn't the best pre-bedtime reading – what little sleep I did get was plagued by dreams of crashing through the fence at the bottom of Shooters Hill and doubts that I could actually complete a marathon only six weeks after my first wheelchair-racing training session.

5.45 a.m.: I head down to breakfast with my box of Raisin Wheats, which were the only thing I could keep down before varsity lacrosse matches, so I'm hoping the same will apply to the London Marathon. A lovely American lady who has completed over fifty marathons comes and sits at my table with her husband and between them they make me feel a whole lot more comfortable about the race, yet simultaneously make it glaringly clear just how out of my depth I am.

6.30 a.m.: Waiting in the early morning light for the bus to the start, it suddenly hits me just what I've let myself in for. The other athletes look so strong, confident and relaxed whereas I'm already panicking. If I pull out now will Stoke Mandeville NSIC still get all the sponsorship money people have so generously donated to replace the sports hall that was demolished just after I left? Brian helps quell the worst of my nerves by keeping the chattier recreational racers away from me and sending me to a seat near the back of the bus where I can look out of the window and pick up tips from the talk of the more experienced racers. I'm also feeling a little unprepared as the organizers wouldn't let me wear my 'Stoke Mandeville NSIC' lycra so I'm having to race in the dirty training kit I wore the day before, which threw me somewhat.

6.45 a.m.: OK, this whole crazy ordeal is worth it for the cool factor of being escorted along the Embankment by police motorbikes and having the traffic lights changed to green as we approach. With Air Traffic on my iPod I'm a little calmer and actually starting to feel excited about finally getting the chance to emulate my dad and my godmother and do a London Marathon.

7.15 a.m.: Getting off the bus at the blue start area, the excitement builds seeing the fields of fun-runners in their fancy dress. The atmosphere is buzzing and there's a continual hum of chat and laughter as the wheelchair athletes are directed into the start tent. Brian once again is a life-saver, pumping my tyres for me and instructing me on where to warm up. The lady from breakfast lends me a pair of glove liners that will apparently help prevent too many blisters from my rather low-tech gloves made from a pair of gardening gloves and lots of athletic tape. The highlight, though, has to be when multi-Paralympic medallist Kurt Fearnley comes up to talk to me. [I recently reminded him of that when we flew back from racing in Switzerland together and he said he thought I was a proper girlie girl and really shy – that shows how nervous and in awe of him I was, as shy is not usually the first word you'd use to describe me and girlie girl wouldn't be near the top either!]

8 a.m.: Warming up along the road beside the tent is pretty hairy stuff. I hadn't realized how fast the elite guys go and I've never seen so many wheelchair racers let alone had to navigate between them to prepare for the biggest sporting event of my life. I'm really glad when the marshals usher us through the barriers to line up for the start.

8.15 a.m.: I'm now lined up in a grid that could double as a who's who of wheelchair racing. There's Amanda McGrory and Shelly Woods, who I watched compete in the 5 k race in Beijing that first got me interested in wheelchair athletics. David Weir is giving an interview to the BBC on the start line. Ernst van Dyk is waving to the cameras. And there I am in the middle of the grid with lots of guys who are far faster than me on the rows behind. I hope I don't get in their way too much.

8.20 a.m.: Bang! The gun goes and the 2009 London Wheelchair Marathon is under way. For the first half-hour I'm feeling great and when I pass through the 10 km marker I see my time is a personal best over that distance. This bodes well as Michelle, the race organizer, said in the tent that we had to hit eleven miles by one hour ten minutes, which meant I had to PB over the first half of the race.

9.19 a.m.: I hit eleven miles after fifty-nine minutes – after this point I can't be pulled out of the race, so as long as I don't hit the dreaded 'wall' I'm on my way to finishing my first marathon. The whole way around the course so far I've been in a state of euphoria that I'm actually competing in this amazing event, and hearing people shout my name as I pass by the crowds is such a confidence boost (even if I can't tell who it is shouting in the sea of faces!).

10.20 a.m.: After two hours of pushing it's suddenly like someone's sapped all the energy out of me and I really start to worry that I'm not going to finish the race. Coming up the small rise after one of the tunnels I worry that I won't even get to the top of the hill. [Tanni, who was watching my progress on the monitors in the BBC studio where she was commentating on the wheelchair race, saw me crying as I emerged and told me afterwards she didn't think I'd manage another mile after that. There were eight more to go before I would reach the finish line. There's something totally unmatchable about the London Marathon atmosphere to me, maybe it's because it's my 'home' city or maybe it's the quarter of a million people lining the streets that gives it such an electric vibe, but either way I don't think I could have pulled out of the race even when I felt like my arms were on fire and my shoulders and neck had cramped up so badly that I couldn't lift my head to look above the ground.]

11.30 a.m.: Coming around the final bend with the London Eye behind me I can see the 800 m to go mark in the distance. Pushing up The Mall with my speed in single figures, feeling as though that last kilometre is another twenty-six miles, I'm suddenly joined by Rose, Izzie and Ceci on my right-hand side, running alongside me down The Mall. It's difficult to describe the effect having them there has on me. It feels like after all the months of rehab and time spent feeling miserable at uni since I'd gone back for my final year

I have finally put my injury behind me and found a new focus for my life. Having three of my best friends there who have gone through every second of the transition with me is really special. After a few hundred metres they are ushered back behind the barriers but they spur me on to get to the end.

11.37 a.m. and 37 seconds: Finally I cross the finish line. The officials are trying to get me out of the way as quickly as possible to allow the runners who have started to come through to get past but I can barely push the chair. I may have come in last place by a large margin and finished well outside the cut-off time for the elite race but it feels like the biggest victory I've achieved in any area of my life.

11.45 a.m.: I'm out of my racing chair in the wheelchair finishers' tent and most of the elite athletes have already left. Somehow my mum manages to get hold of two VIP passes so she and my sister arrive in the finishing area. It is a pretty tearful reunion – I think they feel the same as I do: that this marks the start of my new life in a wheelchair after six months of transition from able-bodied student to disabled athlete.

12 p.m.: We finally make it through the crowds to the meet-and-greet area where I find Georgie, Selina and some of the team I competed with at the Inter Spinal Unit Games the week before, as well as my school friends, my friend Rachael from uni, and my godmother and cousin. By this time I'm feeling pretty euphoric as a result of the sugar high from eating the Mars bars Mum brought so it's a pretty excitable meet and greet! Everyone keeps saying how proud they are of me but by this point my euphoria at finishing the London Marathon is starting to be replaced by frustration that I was so much slower than the elite female wheelchair athletes.

1 p.m.: Dad's been waiting in the car, so Mum, Fi and I head back to rescue him. As he puts my race chair in the car he points out that the brake is jammed on as the screw has slipped – that might explain the sudden difficulty I had after two hours of pushing. I'm not sure Ian's ever going to let me live this one down! On the car journey home my brain is buzzing and I can't quite believe that I've just completed the London Marathon less than a year after my injury. I'm already looking forward to next year, though. I'm going to knock an hour off my time.

It really meant a lot that the Stoke Mandeville Spinal Games team came up to London on marathon day to meet me at the finish. It was a pretty emotional event in any case as I'd intended to run the fun run but was instead racing in the elite wheelchair race just six weeks after my first training session and nine months after becoming paralysed. Having the people who had been through the shock of becoming disabled with me as well as my family, my closest school friends, who spent so much time visiting me the summer after I had the accident, and some of my university friends all together again in Green Park was really special. For me completing the London Wheelchair Marathon was a real turning point as it proved to everyone that I'm just as able to do sport and achieve whatever I set my mind to as I ever was.

9

Hitting the Track

The start of my first track season was a little haphazard as it coincided with my finals at Oxford University. Finals are a tough time for any student, let alone a student doing joint honours who has also spent the past three terms adapting to life in a wheelchair. Despite the risks I'd taken with both my dissertation and my extended essay – covering topics that were very close to my heart and actually using myself as one of the sources – I was adamant I didn't want to take up any offers of extra time for my written papers or 'sympathetic marking' to allow for my time in hospital. Since my accident I had become a lot more focused and I wanted to see what I could do academically without any allowances being made for my new disability. After all, I get so frustrated when people patronize me or assume that I'm mentally disabled just because I'm in a chair – it would have been hypocritical to play the disability card for my finals.

To be honest I was quite looking forward to being one of the 'finalists' who were so revered in the Magdalen College library. For the past two years when I was cramming for my end of year exams I'd seen them sitting at the big tables by the windows on the top floor, working at all hours of the day and night surrounded by their illicit sweets and coffee cartons, and now it was my turn. Then came problem number one – top floor. Stairs. No problem – my friends would join me on the ground floor, I was certain. However, unfortunately the flight of large uneven stone steps up to the library entrance prevented me from even getting into the building. They had no handrail for me to pull myself up on and were too high to attempt on my bum without a rail. I'm a very sociable person and I hate being on my own, so that final term at Oxford, where I was confined to studying alone in my room, was one of the most miserable times of my life. It sounds crazy but it was far worse than the previous summer in hospital and it has clouded my memories of the university since then, as despite the best efforts of all the Magdalen staff and my department professors I had to spend what should have been the most memorable term of my degree studying in solitude. I'm not surprised my sister didn't want to study there after the amount I must have moaned to her on my regular trips home to escape the monotony of my college room!

Thanks to my rather intense studying arrangements I got through journal articles at an alarming rate and was desperate for any escape from my room. My role as Vice-Chair of the Magdalen College Commemoration

Ball, an incredible event with 1800 guests and a budget of £250,000, kept me pretty busy but I needed an outlet for all my pent-up energy. For most people, training drops fairly dramatically when they have exams, but for me it went up. I'd have been happy to go round and round the Iffley Road track until I'd completed a marathon if it meant a few hours away from my desk! My neuroscience exams started fairly early in the term, then I had a break of a few weeks in which I probably studied a lot less than I should have thanks to the proximity of the Commemoration Ball, and then I finished the term with my psychology exams, each three hours long. It's a tradition for Oxford students to wear a white carnation to their first exam, pink for all the middle ones and red for the final one. The story goes that Oscar Wilde wore a white carnation for his first exam, then left it in a vase of red-coloured water, so when he took it out for every subsequent exam it had become redder and redder. This is pinned to the gown of your exam uniform, or 'subfusc' (meaning 'without colour' – it's all black and white). For girls, we had a white shirt, black skirt, tights and shoes and a black velvet ribbon tied around our neck under the distinctive black gown. If you didn't wear the correct uniform you risked being sent out of the exam. In one of my physiology papers a guy was sent back to change his socks as they were brown not black – he therefore missed a large chunk of the time allowed. Another tradition is the 'trashing' of finalists as they leave their last exam, with eggs, squid ink, confetti, baked beans, Champagne; you name it and your so-called friends would be throwing it at you as you came out of Examination Schools with a red carnation pinned to your sub fusc.

My friend Jodie and I had planned a big Hawaiian-themed party at The Oxford Retreat, a bar and restaurant where I used to work, to celebrate our birthdays on the Saturday of my final exam and I was so excited about getting to catch up with all the friends I'd been unable to see while we were cramming for finals. Unfortunately a few weeks before the big day Ian told me it was the Grand Prix athletics meet at Stoke Mandeville that weekend and I needed to be there. My first race was the 1500 m at 3 p.m. so I had to declare by 2 p.m. and I would only finish my final psychology paper ('Pathologies of Belief', one of the toughest but most interesting of my options) at 12.30 p.m. It was a one-hour drive away so that meant I had about half an hour to get from the hall, out of the Examination Schools and into my car. As a result my trashing was a pretty quick affair and unlike the previous year, when I'd had a squid placed on my head, my friends were nice enough just to cover me in Champagne and glitter and accessorize me with balloons, a tiara and some Hawaiian necklaces. With promises I'd be back that evening to celebrate, I sped off towards Stoke Mandeville, still in my sub fusc under which I'd put on my lycra crop top that morning in anticipation of racing.

I must have looked a very strange sight zooming into registration with seconds to spare in a black suit with a gown, a tiara and lots and lots of glitter among all the athletes and coaches in their sportswear. I also smelt like an alcoholic thanks to the Champagne shower, so all in all it earned me some fairly strange looks. Unsurprisingly, I came last in the 1500 m with a time of which I would have been ashamed had I been less exhausted. The adrenaline that had carried me through the nights of cramming and the seemingly endless train of essay papers requiring me to scribble furiously for six hours a day ran out somewhere in the first 200 m of the race and I could barely lift my arms by the end. My performance that day definitely made an impression though – not due to the speed or finesse with which I raced, but because for the next few weeks the track was covered in glitter! After I'd finished racing for the day I wanted to go back to Oxford for the post-finals party but was advised (or commanded!) that this wasn't a good idea with more races the next day, so my finals celebration was an alcohol-free Chinese with Brian, Ian, Tanni and their daughter Carys, followed by an early night. That was my first real experience of the sacrifices you have to make to be an athlete and it was a good lesson to learn, but I have to say that if I could go back and choose again I'd have missed the track meet and stayed in Oxford to celebrate the end of one of the most important chapters of my life. I put athletics first all the time for four years, but now experience has taught me that you don't need to go to every race on the calendar and there does need to be some sort of balance or you end up having no other life, and this is detrimental to training and racing as you start to resent it. I'll never get back the experience of finishing finals, and not getting to celebrate with all the other students made the final weeks of my last term in Oxford a little out of sync with my friends, who were all reminiscing about their trashings and the post-finals parties.

After term ended I went to Europe for my first experience of international racing with Ian and Tanni. We drove to the German National Championships, which was one of the strangest meets I've been to so far. Not only did you have to either throw your chair down a flight of stairs then follow it on your bum, or try to traverse an insanely steep slope accessed from the main road to even get on the track, but you then had to find a way back out if you needed the bathroom or food and drink. On a couple of occasions when navigating the slope, I had to choose between falling out of my day chair but saving my racing chair or letting go of the racing chair and risking it smashing into the barrier below and getting damaged. A great venue for a disability track meet! It got worse once you got onto the track – I was put in lane eight for one of my races and was confronted by a sand pit as I came round the bend! It filled half my lane so I had no choice but to jerk over to lane seven. Thankfully I was so far behind the other girls, mainly due to my inexperience and partially as I was racing as a T54, having not yet been classified internationally, that there was no risk of my lane change causing a crash! Aside from these slightly unusual venue attributes this first track meet proved fairly representative of most international meets – held at a track outside of town in a fairly dingy area, no possibility of any sightseeing or even decent restaurants to eat in, but tons of fun thanks to the hundreds of athletes of all nationalities milling around the area.

From Germany we headed straight over to Switzerland, where Ian was coaching the Great Britain U23 team at the Junior World Championships held in Nottwil. Since that trip Nottwil has been one of my favourite places to train, and Switzerland has been one of my favourite countries. Everything is so accessible and clean, not to mention beautiful (plus I met my boyfriend there!). For a tourist Nottwil would quickly be branded one of the most boring places on Earth – it has one bar, a decent Thai restaurant and a 'beach' made of grass at the side of a small swimming area in Lake Sempach. However, it is also the home of the Swiss Paraplegic Centre (SPZ), which is Switzerland's far superior equivalent of Stoke Mandeville NSIC. Inside the Paraplegic Centre is a restaurant with a wide range of healthy and unhealthy food to keep any athlete or patient happy, a room full of rollers for indoor wheelchair athletics training and a hall full of table-tennis tables to keep us amused between races. Adjacent to the hospital is a track and two nice hotels where athletes are housed for the duration of competitions, and the roads looping the lake provide a smooth and straight half-marathon distance training route. It's unsurprising when you take all this into account that some of the best athletes in the world use the SPZ as their training base!

Although I'd raced a few times on the track in the UK, by the time we headed to Switzerland I hadn't met many of the GB athletes as I'd been totally focused on trying to work out where I was supposed to be and in what I was supposed to be racing. And to be honest I didn't think that these superconfident people in their red, white and blue lycra would give a newbie like me the time of day. As it turns out, I was right. Although I wasn't competing at the Junior World Championships the athletes were my age and I'd hoped I could learn a lot from the British team and also get some good training in with Ian. That hope was dashed about an hour after we arrived at the SPZ. We went into the hospital building for a much-needed hot drink after the long drive (where my addiction to Caotina hot chocolate started!) and the team were all there laughing and joking in the restaurant. Tanni took me over and introduced me and I can honestly say the athletes were unwelcoming to the point of being rude. Barely anyone spoke to me, except to say, 'You can't eat with us, it's for athletes only.' It turned out to be a glimpse of what was to come for the next week. Thankfully I was close to one of the Swedish athletes and was actually staying out in Nottwil for an extra week after he finished racing to train with the Swiss athletes, so he provided many introductions to far more friendly Australian, American and European athletes. It's funny – none of the athletes on the GB junior team that year seem to remember meeting me and some of them are now friends of mine but those first impressions from that time in Nottwil have stayed with me. As a result I tried to be polite and welcoming whenever I met new athletes.

What surprised me most about the athletes at the Junior World Championships was how young everyone seemed. That might sound obvious as it was a junior event, but even the U23s behaved to my eyes like kids. One of their favourite activities seemed to be holding the back of each other's chairs and playing a weird game of what looked like being a train. I can't imagine doing that with a group of my university friends of the same age. I have to admit that after a few days I started to totally regress when with the U23 athletes too – although I couldn't bring myself to join in that train game! As soon as competition is over though, the vibe changes to Freshers' Week and it turns into a mass party in whatever country everyone's in at the time. This is such a release after the stress of needing to be able to perform at your best for every track event over two to four days and sometimes even a marathon on top of that spread over a week.

10

A Journey through Sports

The summer after I finished school was a haze of garden parties and sunbathing but I made sure to run every day. My parents' house is surrounded by countryside so I would jog through the fields and the woods until I was exhausted and then turn around and force myself to run home as a way to keep up my fitness and ready myself to trial for the Blues lacrosse and modern pentathlon teams when I got to Oxford University. Once I got to Oxford and started playing for the women's and mixed lacrosse teams I continued to run around Addison's Walk, a woodland trail in Magdalen College, most mornings or go for a swim. Each lacrosse team practised twice a week so on four afternoons I would jog over to the University Parks and play two hours of lacrosse. I also worked out on the cross-trainer in the gym a few days a week for an hour and we had fitness sessions early Friday morning and Tuesday evening, and on Saturday and Wednesday afternoons in the season we had matches at universities around the country. So I was pretty active, but I trained for enjoyment rather than to be the fittest and strongest I could be. A lot of my training was what I would now call 'steady state' – moderately raised heart rate endurance-type fitness.

There's no doubt that the fitness and strength I picked up through my sporty schedule in the first two years of Oxford helped me to rehab very quickly after I broke my back. Not only was I fit and strong enough to lift and push myself at least enough to be more independent than most people are a month after a spinal injury, but also I had the mentality to make me continue to train as soon as I was allowed out of bed. I joined the gym at Stoke Mandeville Stadium as soon as I was able to push myself back up the hill to the hospital so that I could use slightly more modern equipment than that available in the archery room at the hospital. Whenever the handbikes were available in the physio gym I would jump on for a while in an attempt to lose some of the weight I'd gained in hospital and build up my arm strength to make moving myself around without my legs a little easier. On top of that every afternoon was spent playing various wheelchair sports or doing wheelchair skills, so all in all my eleven weeks at Stoke Mandeville NSIC were a lot of fun and the perfect preparation for continuing with sport after leaving hospital.

Watching the Beijing Paralympic Games in hospital gave me another goal to train for on top of just improving my upper-body strength so I could be an independent wheelchair user. Although I was very active during my time playing university lacrosse I knew I was not going to continue with the sport after I left so I didn't have any particular reason to push myself too far out of my comfort zone in the gym or while out running. However, after seeing the excitement of the Paralympic Games all of a sudden I had a very real and very challenging goal to attain. I wanted to be there. More than that, I wanted to be one of those strong, fit elite athletes who seemed to leave their disability at the gate to the stadium and showcase their incredible ability at the track, on the pitch or in the pool. I never expected that I'd be in with a shout of competing at the London Paralympic Games in only four years' time, but I decided after watching the track athletics that I was going to represent Great Britain at least once in my life.

Then I just had to choose a sport, and after brief dalliances with rowing, fencing and throwing, track athletics became my weapon of choice. The thrill of going at speed down hills beat anything any of those other sports could offer, and I liked being able to train on roads wherever I wanted rather than having to go to a specific facility like the rowing and fencing teams. I was lucky to be coached by Ian Thompson from my very first training session. Initially he agreed to coach me for just the six weeks running up to my first London Marathon but two and a half years on he was still my coach. Having a coach like Ian gave me opportunities that most new athletes would never get. Not only did he write me detailed weekly programmes and demand a detailed diary of my health and training sessions every day; he also ensured that I was entered into every necessary race and tapered my training in preparation for them. Being thrown in at the deep end in this way may not be the best approach for some people, but for me it was important to see how the elite athletes behaved both on and off the track. It enabled me to learn from them and therefore improve at a far faster rate than I would have had I remained in my comfort zone racing in Britain, where it's easy to get a false sense of how good you are due to the smaller pool of female athletes to compete against.

In order for me to be able to race internationally and not disgrace myself any more than absolutely necessary, Ian set me a pretty full-on programme. If I thought that training for my A2 PEP was hard, this was a whole new level. I trained twice a day, six days a week, doing one session in the chair and another either conditioning or in the gym. These sessions were not a case of simply doing the allotted time or pushing until I was tired. I was required to push myself hard but also to train smart. At the end of an interval session in the chair I would often feel as though I'd done a full bleep test and even steady-state recovery sessions could be a killer on the arms as I'd push anything up to thirty miles. For the first time training became the main focus of my life and I had to turn down invitations to spend weekends or even days away with friends or family if it meant missing sessions. I rarely went out at night as more often than not I'd have to do a training session the next morning. Drinking was out of the question and it didn't take long for the novelty of being the only sober one in the place to wear off.

Although shifting my focus so that training and racing came above pretty much everything else in my life was a big change, I have to admit I miss the simplicity of it. In weeks when I was not racing, my life followed a steady routine of training morning and afternoon, eating healthily, resting between sessions and getting a good night's sleep. Sometimes I got frustrated that I was not able to see my friends very often, especially in the summer when I was often away racing at least two weeks a month. Pretty soon I was also spending one month in two in Canada to train, so on my day off when I was in the UK I'd try to spend time with my friends and family. In between I'd talk to my friends via email or Skype all the time so it didn't seem so bad if I didn't see them as much as I used to. I also made tons of new friends around the world through athletics so spending months at a time away from home didn't ever feel lonely.

What tends to shock a lot of people is that Paralympic athletes train like any able-bodied elite athlete. Different coaches have different approaches, but neither Ian nor my second coach Rick make any allowances for their athletes being disabled. Both of them were elite wheelchair athletes so they have first-hand experience of what training works when it comes to winning races. Around where I used to live the roads are very busy but I was lucky to have Stoke Mandeville Stadium less than fifteen minutes from my house so I used the track there a lot. It's a Mondo track just like they use in the Paralympics so it should be a lot faster than training on the standard Tartan tracks most schools and sports centres have. Or at least it would be if the buildings hadn't been constructed with such a layout that they form a wind tunnel that makes you feel as though you're going to be blown off the track! One particular track meet at Stoke, the officials had to turn a blind eye to athletes leaving their lanes in the corners as the wind was gusting so hard that we couldn't keep the chairs in lane at all. It made for good training, though, as I got resistance into the wind and over-speed practice with the tailwind, and now my training has stepped down a level the tailwind provides a great chance for a break!

Resistance training in the chair is really useful so although my focus was the track sprints I still hill trained at least once a week. There's a 5 km climb up a cycle path just outside Aylesbury that I used for hill sprints as I didn't have to worry about traffic when travelling at well over twenty miles an hour on the way back down. I did scare the odd dog who had escaped from its owner though! Most of my workouts in the chair were very high intensity so I'd warm up for at least 5 km before I started and take an old inner tube with me to stretch with during the sessions. I often got people coming up and asking me if I needed help to change my tyre, which was very kind, but when I explained that I was just using the tube to stretch my pecs and arms they did look at me rather strangely. After snapping far too many expensive gym stretching bands I'd much rather use the inner tubes that Continental Tyres gave me as part of their sponsorship! On paper, hill climbing should be pretty hard work, which it is, but I actually quite liked the pain as it's totally different to the lactic acid build-up you get sprinting on the track. The margins of improvement were also much more obvious and I liked being able to see the results of each session immediately. In the winter especially my training load was so heavy and the sessions were so intense that it was easy to get dispirited by my top speeds on the track. My time training in Canada helped a lot to keep me motivated and positive as I could see first-hand that the other athletes I was training with had the same gripes but that our coach had no concerns.

Three times a week I used to spend an hour and a half to two hours in the gym working on strength in the winter, and power in the spring and summer. I used to hate this part as I didn't want 'man arms', but after a while I started to get a bit of a kick out of guys going to the machines right after I used them and having to decrease the load on the bar. Winter strength sessions especially were painfully hard and pretty boring so I needed small pleasures like that to keep me going! I had to watch out, though, as I managed to disconnect my sternum using the seated row machine. I had it loaded up nearly to the maximum available and didn't tense my core before pulling on the bar. I felt a bit of a pop where the vertical support was pressed into the centre of my ribcage and it hurt a little but I didn't think anything of it and finished the set. That afternoon I met Helene, my rowing friend, for coffee and mentioned it to her. She was a little more worried than me and suggested I saw a doctor for a scan, which I did. The X-ray showed I'd done a pretty good job of dislocating my sternum and the doctor could actually get his fingers between the cartilage and the bone in the centre of my ribcage. Needless to say that made for a painful few weeks of training! I can't say I miss gym sessions now they're not a part of my workout routine.

In addition to the weights work I did in the gym I also did conditioning sessions twice a week using body-weight exercises to improve my core strength and work on speed and power. I joked when I was competing that these sessions were to make me look like an athlete as they included 250–300 'sit-ups', but now I appreciate having been introduced to them as they help my body to retain some sort of resemblance to how it was when I was racing! As I don't have the use of my lower abs sit-ups look more like I'm jerking around on the floor writhing in pain but I like to think they must be doing something to keep my stomach toned. I also still do my rotator cuff exercises every day – I'm very prone to twinges in my shoulders even when I'm only working out once a day and pushing to and from work, and after two serious shoulder injuries while I was racing I'd rather avoid a third.

In the winter we worked on base fitness as a good foundation of endurance is needed whatever distance you race over. My best events were the 200 m and 400 m but I started the season with longer road races in the spring as they provided a good test of how effective my training was over the winter. The London Marathon is my favourite event so I hope to race it again at a more recreational level in the future. With the snow in Canada I often spent weeks in winter on the rollers, which are effectively the equivalent of a treadmill for racing chairs, albeit less advanced – essentially they consist of a cylinder that rotates as you push the back wheels and a clamp that holds the front wheel in place. I used to set them up in front of the TV and watch dance movies as it's difficult to hear the speech over the sound of my plastic gloves hitting the carbon-fibre disc wheels I use for endurance sessions. The *Step Up* trilogy make great roller movies as there's lots to look at and as long as you can vaguely hear the music you won't miss anything. The problem with this method, though, was that I would easily get distracted and realize that for the past ten minutes I'd been pushing so easily that my heart rate had dropped as I'd been so engrossed in the action on screen. This was a problem while I was racing as a professional athlete, but now I love to have movie sessions on the rollers as it stops me feeling lazy for sitting around watching movies! I also still love going out on Sunday mornings as the sun is coming up to train along the Oxford Road with fields on either side of me or in Richmond Park without having any pressure to keep looking ahead and remember to keep good pushing technique. This allows me to finally enjoy the gorgeous view clearly rather than through a haze of sweat and exhaustion.

In April 2011 I gave up my role as a Licensing Executive in the Commercial Team at the London Organising Committee of the Olympic and Paralympic Games (LOCOG). It was a scary move as I loved my job and was lucky to have a great deal more responsibility and variety in my role than most recent graduates, not to mention the perks that come from working with companies like adidas, especially as an athlete. And for someone with a Union Jack fetish like mine the freebies from my licensees were pretty addictive! Bex, one of my friends in the licensing team, Photoshopped me onto a spoof cover of *Sport* magazine when I left with the tagline 'Savlon shares soar as Emerson announces training schedule', so that gives a little bit of an idea of how much training I was doing around a full-on job plus a two-hour commute each way to Canary Wharf. The three days a week I trained twice a day I got up at 4.45 a.m. to get a training session in before catching the 6.24 a.m. tube up to London, then went straight from the Tube station after work to Stoke Mandeville Stadium, arriving around 8 p.m. and finishing training by 9.30 p.m. And I still had to cook dinner when I got home.

In between training sessions I worked on apparel, sports equipment and soft furnishings licensing for London 2012. I had the opportunity to go through every stage of the licensing process with various licensees. The design and marketing phases were my favourite, but I also enjoyed the appointment process as it was always nice to hear how enthusiastic the applicant companies were about the Games.

Looking back I'm not entirely sure how my body put up with the demands I placed on it. Every athlete knows the principle that rest time is when the benefits from training set in. So if you don't rest you get very little benefit from training. However, if you don't train you get no benefits at all and the work you've put in is quickly reversed, so as I had to have a job to pay for my athletics (and other boring things like food and petrol) this rather hectic schedule was pretty unavoidable. Thankfully, after a fourth-place finish at the 2010 London Marathon and four medals at the U23 World Championships I picked up enough sponsorship for me to give up my full-time job if I lived at my parents' to avoid paying rent. This gave me the incredible freedom of being able to work part-time on various projects that fitted in around my training schedule, including becoming an Ambassador for WheelPower, a Trustee for SportsAid and doing media interviews and consultancy.

My coaching set-up wasn't ideal for the first three years I raced as I lived five hours away from Ian, and being such a sociable person I started to get very dispirited once I gave up my job at LOCOG, as I could go weeks without seeing another athlete outside competition season. I got to the point where I wouldn't want to get out of bed in the morning as all I had to look forward to every day was two training sessions on my own because my friends were all studying and working miles away from where I lived. I also caught a virus at the end of the 2011 track season, probably as a result of all the travelling I was doing with very little time to recover from the flight before I had to go out training in whatever country I'd landed in. I felt exhausted the whole time. As a result I performed far below the level expected from me in the final road races of the year, the Great North Run and the Berlin Marathon in 2011. This meant that I didn't achieve the London 2012 Paralympic qualification standard in the Berlin Marathon so I was feeling very dispirited. One day I was talking to my boyfriend Kyle, who I met racing in Switzerland in 2011 and who was on the Canadian wheelchair track team, and he asked if I'd like to come and train with the Cyclones, who are the wheelchair road and track club he trained with in Saskatoon. His coach had extended an open invitation to me to train with them so I booked my flights and took off for a month in Canada. By the time I left, my top speed on the rollers had increased by nearly 4 mph. I don't know whether it was just having a coach present or having people to train with and compete against, or even just that I was happier in Canada as I got to see Kyle and was constantly surrounded by friends, but training there made sport feel fun again.

11

Sport for All:
Charities and Mentoring

When I was a kid I looked up to athletes far more than I looked up to celebrities in other fields. At weekends, before my sister was born, Mum would put me in the seat on the back of her bike and we'd go on family bike rides, and when she had a tennis or a squash game planned with her friend Carol I would be sat at the side of the court in my carrier next to her daughter Kat, who is a few months older than me, and we would jabber away in our own language for hours. As we grew up this progressed into joining my dad's karate classes and playing hockey with our miniature sticks at the side of the Astroturf when he had training or a match. Being allowed to sit in the sports club bar after the match and drink our ginger beers (which we were convinced were alcoholic) was the icing on the cake. As pre schoolers Kat and I were inseparable, going to swimming class, ballet class and the sports club together every day. I think this helped me to stay interested in sport as she was always far more talented than me and being far more athletically built she excelled at pretty much everything. At this time I had a huge covering of puppy fat so had it not been for Kat's confidence and eternal kindness in partnering the fat kid I would probably have refused to put on my leotard or swimsuit and go to class. When we reached school age we were sent to different primary schools and I refused even to get changed for PE, which proves the influence she had over me! By a weird twist of fate the companies we now work for are housed in the same small building in London, so we still get lots of opportunities to see each other.

As a result of having parents who stressed the importance of being active so much it's unsurprising that I quickly became a big sports fan. I loved to watch rugby and tennis, and quickly learned that while I was never the best at any sport there were none that I couldn't get by in (aside from ballet, which I quit fairly young due to having absolutely no talent there whatsoever). Holidays were spent at tennis camps with Kat or riding camps as my mum was an enthusiastic horse rider and I was lucky enough to have a horse on loan through my teens and competed for the local Riding Club and Pony Club at area finals. Probably as a result of the strong influence my parents had on my participation in sport it's not surprising that the athletes I looked up to were more from their generation. Paula Radcliffe and Steve Redgrave were always praised in our house, and rugby players such as Lawrence Dallaglio, Lewis Moody, Mike Tindall, Ben Cohen, Matt Dawson and Jason Robinson were the type of athlete I looked up to as they were articulate, friendly (off the pitch) and seemed to be the sort of dependable guy you'd want to marry. They were dedicated professionals. In my opinion the footballers who are caught falling out of clubs in the early hours of the morning and having affairs left, right and centre don't strike me as athletes, however much they might get paid for playing their sport.

In addition to the obvious training and racing side of an athlete, I really admire those elite competitors who give something back through coaching or visits to schools. Many able-bodied athletes at the top of their game are treated like celebrities, and as such they can have a big effect on a large number of people. I look up to athletes like Lance Armstrong (regardless of his fall from grace) and Jessica Ennis, who do many things outside of their sport to help people, whether it's Lance through his cancer campaigning or Jessica through her media influence on girls across the country. The first year I raced the London Marathon, six months after I left Stoke Mandeville NSIC, I decided to raise money for WheelPower as they had offered to buy me a racing wheelchair through their Wheel Appeal scheme that provides sports wheelchairs for newly injured and young wheelchair users to help them get into sport. It was a pretty rushed decision as I only qualified for the marathon the month before through sheer luck, or perhaps great judgement by my coach Ian Thompson, but from what I had heard they were a great charity. In six weeks I had raised over £35,000 from friends, family, business associates of my dad, friends of my grandmother and even people I met only briefly at the Spinal Games the week before the London Marathon, who had heard about my somewhat surprisingly quick turnaround, found my JustGiving page and donated.

That was the start of what has become a great involvement with WheelPower. Any success I had in athletics was largely thanks to their Wheel Appeal, which funded the two racing chairs I have owned and aimed to provide 2012 sports wheelchairs to children or newly disabled people by 2012. WheelPower also run camps that allow children to meet other kids with disabilities and various 'Games', such as the Spinal Games that I competed at and camps for amputees and primary- and secondary-school-aged disabled children. I am now an ambassador for the charity, which gives me the opportunity not only to coach at these Games and give many people their first experience of wheelchair racing or handcycling, but also to speak at corporate events and meet lots of really interesting business people.

After giving up full-time work I spent a lot of the time between training sessions when I was in the UK visiting schools to speak at assemblies and teaching variations on Paralympic sports in PE lessons. My adaptation of blind football, where the kids pair up so that each blindfolded person has a sighted guide to lead them to the ball, is a particular favourite, and sitting volleyball always goes down well, too, until bottoms get sore! I really enjoy going into schools and getting to meet the kids and answer their questions. The Friends of King's College Junior School in Wimbledon in particular were very supportive of me, and I had the opportunity to chat to lots of the boys who were very forthcoming with their questions, which I love.

Unlike adults, who usually don't ask the questions they'd really like to know the answers to for fear of seeming rude, children, especially young boys, don't have that worry. My favourite questions so far have been how do I get my chair onto the bed to sleep and where do I put my legs when I cut them off to get into my racing chair! When I'm out and about in town I get a lot of children running up and staring at me, then going back to their embarrassed mothers to ask why I'm in a buggy, which is very cute. The way the parents react is interesting to watch, too. Some get angry at their child and tell them off for running over to me and a lot avoid the question. I don't think that really helps children to understand and become accepting of disability though, so I'd much rather they do what the minority do and either bring their child over to ask me or tell them to ask me themselves. I've had a lot of practice at explaining what happened to me in a way that doesn't upset even sensitive young children. In fact, I think I'm getting too good at making being in a wheelchair sound fun – one parent emailed me after I visited her son's school to tell me he'd asked for a wheelchair for Christmas!

Going into primary schools to teach children about disability and the Paralympics is one of my favourite parts of being a disabled athlete. I also really enjoy speaking at corporate events. What I'm less comfortable with is the areas in between. The first time I was asked to speak at a sixth-form conference at my old school, Wycombe Abbey, I was terrified! Knowing how judgemental we all were of the many speakers we listened to at our weekly Friday-night lectures I was fully prepared to be slaughtered by the extremely intelligent students I'd be addressing. To make matters worse I was asked to accompany my talk with a PowerPoint presentation, which I hate as it turns what should hopefully be an inspirational discussion into a lecture. Kyle came with me to Wycombe Abbey as he was intrigued to see inside a British boarding school and to hear me give one of my speeches, but the whole way there I was so nervous I couldn't stop babbling. Crazy really – I'm totally comfortable getting up in front of hundreds of accomplished business people and speaking unaided for as long as they ask me to, but tell me to talk to a theatre full of late-teenage girls and their teachers with the aid of a presentation and I'm a wreck. When the majority of the seats in the tiered auditorium I was so used to sitting in were filled, my old Head of Clarence House, Mrs Tear, introduced me and I was so taken aback by how nice yet honest she was about my schooldays that I totally fluffed my welcome to the students. My opening line went something like:

'I know this is a leadership conference but I don't really lead, I sort of just follow what my coach tells me to do so I hope I'll provide some light relief after lunch before you go back to learning about leadership.'

Bad start. Not only was I talking total rubbish, I also totally failed to realize that I'd been invited to speak at the conference because the teachers hoped that I could lead the girls by example through showing them how far I'd come since breaking my back to now being an international athlete. Whether or not my day-to-day job involved leadership was, I think, fairly irrelevant. It wasn't one of my finest speeches – I was so determined to prove to the girls that I did deserve to be taking up their time that I'm sure I came across brash and arrogant. The nerves went once I got into the flow of the talk but I was still very relieved to get to the end of my much-detested slides and move on to the unscripted Q and A session. The girls had some really great questions and it was a welcome change to be asked detailed questions about my sport, from classification to the place of the Paralympics in relation to the Olympics instead of the usual queries I get about my disability. It was great to go back to school and see my teachers, too, and showing Kyle around the sports complex and grounds really reminded me how lucky I am to have had the chance to study there. The last two years I've returned to give more speeches at Wycombe, and thankfully I don't panic anymore!

Being an athlete opened a lot of doors for me away from sport. Through a colleague at LOCOG I was introduced to Hanah Burgess, the Head of Strategy and Disability at Leonard Cheshire Disability, a charity that works in the UK and over fifty other countries to provide services and campaign for disabled people. She also went to Wycombe Abbey so we hit it off right away and I became involved with Leonard Cheshire's events team and their drive to make running events in the UK more accessible. I also worked with them to provide a basic-level training guide for wheelchair users looking to take part in their first fun run and a blog with monthly training tips that will hopefully help with the motivational side of training.

I'm pretty passionate about getting disabled people of all ages into sport. For anybody sport is not only important for health reasons but is also a great way to meet people and have fun at the same time as losing weight and increasing fitness. For disabled people, though, it's even more important to exercise but it is far harder for wheelchair users to take part in sport. Compared to the size of the muscles in the average able-bodied person's legs, arm muscles are tiny. This means that even when they have been built up through years in a wheelchair they will not burn as many calories as leg muscles would during exercise of the same intensity and duration. Put simply, walking around the office burns a lot more calories than wheeling around it. So this means that wheelchair users don't need to eat as much as people who walk. However, this doesn't mean that wheelchair users get less hungry. I put on a stone and a half during my eleven weeks in hospital after breaking my back and becoming a wheelchair user. I was exercising for hours every day both in the physio gym and pool during my rehab sessions and in the sports hall playing wheelchair basketball, hockey and doing fitness sessions. However, I was also still eating the amount I had been before my accident when my legs were burning calories walking around Oxford and running around the lacrosse pitch, so I got fat. What was most worrying for me was that I didn't even notice I was gaining weight. I always teased my friends when they said they'd suddenly gained a stone but now I see how that can happen! One day about two weeks before I was due to be discharged from Stoke Mandeville NSIC I woke up and went into the bathroom to brush my teeth as usual. As I turned to grab my towel I caught sight of my arm in the mirror. I'd expected my arms to bulk up with muscle from all the use they were getting but I never expected them to look how they did then. I had serious bingo wings. Looking closer I noticed my face had become a lot rounder too and there was a definite double chin developing. And at the point my back brace stopped, where there had previously been jutting hipbones that I'd complained were getting bruised by the plastic, there were now wobbly love handles. It was hard enough for me having to adjust from being a tall, slim twenty-year-old who was used to getting a lot of attention from guys to being a wheelchair user who in my opinion at that time would never have another boyfriend, but at least I'd expected to still be able to fit into my old clothes. Now I'd even lost my figure. It was time to do something about this.

When I got back to my bed on the ward I threw out all the chocolate and sweets I'd been brought by visitors. Then I resolved to exercise even more than I already was, starting with daily morning swims at Stoke Mandeville Stadium where I'd become a member so I could use the weights gym to build up my strength with extra sessions outside of those provided by the hospital. Those last few weeks in hospital, it was easy to stick to my new weight-loss regime and although I didn't notice any immediate difference in my body shape my face started to return to its former structure. When I left Stoke Mandeville and went back to Oxford it was a lot harder to eat healthily and exercise, though. As I had the added incentive that I was trying to make it onto the GB adaptive rowing squad I managed to stick to my plan but it wasn't easy. Cooking in the kitchen in my halls was difficult as the surfaces were all very high and I couldn't reach any of the cupboards. I nearly cracked and bought a panini from the sandwich shop next door almost every day. There was also the added distraction of student levels of alcohol to drag me away from my health kick.

Exercising was even harder. Being away from the hospital meant no more organized team sports, so I had to train alone. I went to the Iffley Road gym where I had free membership as an Oxford University Blue a few times in the first week of term but I felt as though everyone was staring at me and wondering why the girl in a wheelchair was trying to do sport among the Blues squad members. I wouldn't go through the doors without some piece of University team kit on in a bid to prove that I deserved to be there, but even then I felt out of place and miserable. My close friend Sarah and I had been members at LA Fitness in Oxford before my accident but I was nervous to go back there. After a few miserable sessions at Iffley Road, though, Sarah convinced me to bite the bullet and text Andy, my old personal trainer, and tell him what had happened. He was understandably shocked when I explained that I was now in a wheelchair but incredibly supportive when I told him I was going to get into Paralympic sport. He developed a training programme specifically tailored to improving my upper-body strength and endurance for rowing that he promised would also shift my excess poundage. It was a slow process and I didn't really notice that I was losing the weight I'd gained around my stomach. However, my arms and shoulders became far more defined so Andy's military-style training must have been helping somehow! I really enjoyed my gym sessions as it was nice to be able to chat to someone sporty now that I wasn't getting to spend time with my lacrosse friends.

As well as working out in the gym, my dad lent me his indoor rowing machine to train on so that I didn't have to endure the stares from all the Blues rowers in the Iffley Road gym. I can understand why they found my rowing training a little strange. Adaptive rowing is really an entirely different sport to its able-bodied equivalent. Both take place on water and involve moving backwards but that's just about where the similarities end. In my adaptive rowing class, the arms-only classification, we used single sculls with two blades as normal, but the boats have floats attached to the side to prevent them from capsizing. The seat is also held stationary and has a high back with straps that go across your hips, stomach and chest to prevent use of any core muscles the athletes may have. The vast majority of the power therefore comes from your biceps, upper back and shoulders. The same seat can be clipped onto a standard ergo for indoor training, which is what I did in the Iffley gym. I began to dread ergo training after only a few days back at Oxford as there's never any chance of finding the gym empty of rowers and I had to go through what I felt at the time was the embarrassment of clipping my 'cripple' seat onto the ergo and pulling with my strange arms-only stroke. Once I had an ergo in my room, though, I was happy to follow the training programme Tom at GB Rowing had given me and I worked out every day.

After I left Oxford and switched to doing athletics I really appreciated how lucky I was to have the option of training with a personal trainer in the gym to learn what exercises are best for wheelchair users and to be able to do my cardiovascular workouts in the comfort of my own home. I still find going into an unfamiliar gym, full of able-bodied people working out, a bit daunting. Not only do I have to contend with the likelihood of the room having steps up or down to it, but once I get in there the majority of weights rooms are very crowded so I usually end up having to move bars and benches out of the way to be able to get to the machines and dumbbells I need. I'm used to getting around the accessibility issues after a few years of grabbing workouts in hotel or public sports centres but I'm not sure I'll ever get used to the confused looks I get from the other people working out there, and especially a lot of the personal trainers working in the gyms. I suppose it does look a bit odd seeing me wheel around the gym with stacks of dumbbells on my lap or lift my legs over the bench in order to sit in the right way to do my workout, but I would expect an onlooker to realize that I should be quite strong as I'm a wheelchair user who can quite plainly push herself around with her arms very easily. Every so often someone will come over and say something along the lines of, 'Try this one, that's too heavy' or 'Would you like me to take some weight off that bar?' It's really nice they want to help but I wouldn't go up to a weedy-looking guy when he's working out and tell him how to do his exercises or give him a lighter weight. It's a little patronizing and slightly insulting!

Training for wheelchair athletics when I was at Oxford, even once I had sorted out my gym access, was a bit of a mission. Gone was the easy routine of rolling out of bed and onto my rowing machine. Instead I needed to find a road or track to train on. The roads around Oxford are very busy and I was not yet fast enough to keep up with the bikes in the cycle lanes so the track at Iffley Road was my best option for training. It is a very prestigious track as Roger Bannister completed the first four-minute mile on that site in 1954 and it is now the home of the Oxford University Athletics Club. I had run there a few times as part of the Cuppers intercollegiate athletics competition every summer and from what I remembered access was as simple as opening the big gates from the road into the sports complex that open directly onto the track. Apparently not. I was told I would have to push my racing chair up the steep switchback ramp to the main entrance, somehow get through the double doors at the top without either my racing chair or the everyday chair I was in slipping back down the steps or the ramp behind me, pass through the entry gate and immediately around a corner so sharp I had to lift my racing chair up to get around it, then through more double doors before I got into the entrance area to the gym and sports hall. Once I got that far it was just a case of negotiating the stretching hall, trying not to run anyone over while they exercised and then out of the double doors and down two steps to the grass beside the track, which posed a barrier in itself when the ground was wet as I would get stuck just feet from the track. It wasn't the easiest set-up to say the least and it was one that had to be repeated before training every day and reversed after each session as I was told there was nowhere to store my racing chair at the huge sports complex. This meant I had no choice but to drive the relatively short distance from Magdalen College to Iffley Road Sports Ground as I couldn't manage pushing two chairs up and down the pavements at that point.

Having finally made it to the track and into my racing chair, most of my sessions doubled up as a lesson in wheelchair handling with the number of times I had to swerve around runners who seemed to have no understanding of the basic rule of every track that you only go anticlockwise around the loop. Racing wheelchairs are set up to turn only left around the corners thanks to the ingenious compensator piece in the steering system that acts as a 'third arm' and holds the front wheel over to the left when a triangular-shaped handle has been hit over to the right. In order to straighten up after the bend you just hit the compensator back to the left and the front wheel is held straight again so you can continue to push around the bends without losing speed. As a result I couldn't just change direction to match the bulk of the runners as I would have had to manually steer around the right-hand corners and therefore spend half of my workout not actually pushing the chair. Instead I had to swerve around not only slow-moving people jogging anticlockwise and the idiotic runners going clockwise directly towards me but also the hurdles that seemed to magically spring up in random positions on the track every few laps. The Athletics Club, who seemed to run sessions there every hour during the day, were not willing to let me have a lane to myself to avoid all this drama so I took to training early in the morning before they were out of bed.

The great thing about training at Stoke Mandeville is that the other people who work out there are completely used to seeing wheelchair users rolling around the place. Nobody bats an eyelash at me throwing myself around the weights room and jumping on and off equipment when I go back there, even when I miss a transfer after exhausting my arms and land on the floor. The guys are great at picking up weights I can't reach and kicking benches out of the way so I can pass, without stopping their workout or making a big deal out of helping me out. The Stadium employs a dedicated personal trainer to focus on disabled members so any wheelchair users or people with other disabilities can receive free personal-training sessions as part of their membership in order to teach them how to lift weights both in their chair and by moving the seats of the integrated machines. The track is also easily accessible and all the runners I've met there have been bright enough to run in the correct direction around the track from the start and are happy to split up the lanes so we're not inter-fering with each other. I tend to avoid the track when Vale of Aylesbury Athletic Club are training as it gets very busy but while I was racing they invited me to train with their 400 m runners to practise my starts and always make space for me if I do have to train during their sessions. It's a little different to my university days! Unfortunately, though, this level of accessibility and acceptance of disability sport is not the norm at sports centres across the country so a lot of wheelchair users are put off exercise before they even start.

I met an incredible lady who had been a wheelchair user since birth and had recently managed to lose six stone in a year after starting to work out with and receive nutrition information from a personal trainer at Stoke Mandeville Stadium. She was amazed at how easy it was to use the gym there and how accommodating everyone was. In the past she had never thought she could do sport due to her disability as she couldn't afford the specialist equipment she needed to do the Paralympic sports she'd seen on TV. In the end she decided that paying membership at Stoke Mandeville Stadium in order to get advice from the per-sonal trainers there was a more cost-effective option. Even so personal training at most gyms is relatively expensive and is not something a lot of wheelchair users, especially those who currently do not exercise, would choose to spend money on every month.

When you're in a wheelchair taking part in sport is not as simple as just putting on a pair of trainers and going for a run. Exercising in an everyday chair can be difficult as when you're pushing fast along a pavement the smallest bump can cause the casters to catch and you to fly forward out of the chair. Trust me, I've done it hundreds of times rushing around London to get to meetings! Handcycling is probably the easiest sport to take up without any real coaching but even the simple bike attachments that clip onto a normal manual wheelchair are far more expensive than a pair of sports shoes. To buy a fully reclined handcycle similar to the ones athletes use in the Paralympics costs around £5000. A racing wheelchair costs about £2500 and coaching is needed to learn the technique. When you add the price of gloves, wheels, repairs and helmets to that initial expense the cost of taking up a wheelchair sport can become prohibitive. For disabled people looking for competitive sports opportunities a lot of wheelchair basketball and rugby clubs have chairs that can be borrowed while users decide if the sport is for them, and the British Handcycling Association and the British Wheelchair Racing Association are sometimes able to loan chairs or bikes for a few months. A few charities like WheelPower and Get Kids Going will accept applications for funding for sports chairs if the user intends to compete in their chosen sport but there is a gap for anyone just looking to use a sports wheelchair or handcycle recreationally a few times a week.

Part of my work with Leonard Cheshire Disability was to find a way around the cost and equipment barriers that many of their service users, who are often far more severely disabled than I am, face when thinking about taking up sport or even just exercise for health. Being overweight carries well-known health risks such as Type 2 diabetes and heart disease. For wheelchair users, especially those with no leg function, it also increases the risk of pressure sores due to the extra weight on the seat bones. When you consider how much harder it is for a wheelchair user to exercise recreationally, and how much easier it is for them to put on weight as they are burning fewer calories than somebody walking around, the threat of obesity becomes very real. The staff at Leonard Cheshire were approached by some of their service users with different disabilities who wished to set themselves a goal to get fit in order to take part in a sports event. They decided to tackle this by setting up Tri Together, a fully inclusive triathlon at Crystal Palace National Sports Centre that allowed able-bodied and disabled people, including those with learning difficulties, mobility impairments and sensory impairments, to take part either in one leg of the triathlon as part of a team or by completing the whole triathlon themselves. The inaugural race in August 2011 was a great success and this is now an annual event growing rapidly and spreading around the country, which is great to see.

One event a year that allows people of mixed disabilities to take part is not nearly enough, though. I worked with Leonard Cheshire to put together a list of fun runs that are fully accessible for people of all disabilities, but the list was sadly not very long and decreases every year. There must be no kerbs as these are a problem for electric wheelchairs. The hills cannot be too steep up or down as manual wheelchair users would struggle to climb them and collide with runners on the downhill. The roads must be wide enough for blind runners to run with guides beside them and for necessary carers to stay alongside learning disabled runners. The roads also need to be smooth enough not to catch wheelchair casters or trip blind runners, and be closed to traffic. A lot of events are very keen to make adjustments so that at least some disabilities can take part, so hopefully the number of opportunities will grow in the future.

Following pressure from many disability groups, the London Marathon tested the idea of having people in everyday wheelchairs complete the fun run rather than the experience only being open to athletes in racing wheelchairs who could achieve the elite cut-off time. One wheelchair user even appealed to the European Court of Human Rights when their fun-run place was taken away after London Marathon discovered that they intended to take part in their wheelchair, so the race organizers asked two wheelchair users to complete the course at the back of the mass of fun-runners in a normal manual wheelchair. After two successful tests the number of people taking part in everyday manual wheelchairs continues to grow. This is a great step forward as racing in the London Marathon has given me some of the best experiences of my life and I believe that everyone should have the opportunity to experience it if they would like to, regardless of disability or athletic prowess. It seems a gross double standard that the most unsporty able-bodied person can run the marathon dressed as a rhino and pushing a pushchair, yet a fit and active wheelchair user who perhaps can't afford a racing wheelchair, or simply does not want to sit in that uncomfortable position for hours on end, is not allowed to take part due to fears that they might impede the runners. But why should the wheelchairs be forced to stay at the back, out of everyone's way? It shouldn't always be wheelchair users having to stay out of the way of runners and not vice versa. I can see why having hundreds of everyday wheelchairs entering the London Marathon could be difficult as runners tend not to look down at wheelchair height when they run, but saying this is a safety problem due to the wheelchair users is not acceptable. The safety issues arise only if runners do not look where they are going.

In addition to the marathon itself, the organizers run the adidas Silverstone Half Marathon, the Bupa London 10 km and many other 5 km races, which are all as well organized as the London Marathon and nearly as exciting to take part in, thanks to the huge number of entrants and festival atmosphere. Silverstone Half Marathon was my first ever race and remains my favourite event of the year; everyday wheelchair users are able to enter the ballot for places and compete in the same way as runners. Having an event like this as a goal is a great motivator to get out and train so Leonard Cheshire Disability is actively encouraging their disabled service users to enter a large run like Silverstone or even a local fun event such as a run, a bike ride or a sponsored swim to give them a tangible reason to start exercising. To support this, a group of athletes including myself put together training guides to give ideas for how to train with whatever equipment you have and how to prevent the injuries that can come about very easily from training too hard or incorrectly. This is a project I really believe in and I hope that it will grow to reach people who are not part of the Leonard Cheshire system and help them to have the confidence to give sport a try. All the information is publically available through the charity's website.

London hosting the Paralympic Games gave an enormous boost to the sponsorship opportunities available for disabled athletes but sadly this didn't continue once the Games were over. Most of my sponsorship agreements ended in 2012 and I had a total change of lifestyle by taking up the place I had deferred for the previous two years at Loughborough University to study for a Master's in International Relations and French. It was great to study such a broad and interesting subject and to use my brain for something other than working out average speeds and heart-rate percentages (and to finally get the first-class degree I didn't quite get the grades for at Oxford)! Being back at university was a bit of a shock to the system as I had to stick to a schedule based around something other than training and remember how to write an essay again, but it was ideal to give me time to make the decision on whether or not I wanted to continue with athletics. I love sport but for me being a full-time athlete is not enough to keep me mentally stimulated. I hated feeling that I was not accomplishing anything useful for the majority of my day once training was over and, even with sponsor commitments and the charity work I did, I missed having structure to my day and looking forward to weekends and holidays as I did when I was working at LOCOG. As an athlete, weekends have little significance and apart from a couple of days off at the end of the season there is no holiday allowance. I trained twice on Christmas Day and raced a marathon on my birthday. Of course the perks of travel and representing my country counteracted this for a while, but in the end there comes a time when you have to grow up and start looking to the long-term future.

I was offered a place to do an MA at Oxford University in African Studies, which is the region that interests me the most, but I turned it down – the sports facilities were still undergoing improvement to make them accessible, so it would have been difficult to keep training in athletics as well as studying for my master's. In hindsight, that was the wrong decision as sport took a back seat for me once I was studying again, but at least the lesser academic workload at Loughborough meant that I could work alongside my master's – and the scholarship they gave me really helped. I couldn't focus my studies on Africa though which was disappointing, but it was great to learn more about US politics instead.

My mother was born and raised in Zambia until the age of twenty and many of her family were driven off their farms in Zimbabwe or had to leave the country as a result of the civil war and Mugabe's officials seizing the farms of white landowners. When I was a kid Mum talked about Africa as though it was a dream world where wide-open spaces and sunshine to play in were unlimited and life was incredibly simple and carefree. I suppose it was to a child growing up on a private estate with household staff in what was then one of the more peaceful African nations. As I became older, though, she shared some of the less glossy details about her childhood and what has stuck with me in particular is her descriptions of trips to local supermarkets with her nanny. The stock on the shelves mainly came from aid packets sent to Zambia by humanitarian charities. That really shocked me and, as much as I hate to admit it, it exemplifies the complaint of critics that aid charities don't actually do any good and any aid they send that is not given directly to the people who need it the most is siphoned off by corrupt governments or rebel forces. Of course, this is not always the case and most charities now implement on the ground bottom-up humanitarian efforts in the place of the old method of dropping aid packets from planes. One day I hope I can take a sabbatical from work and go and actually help one of these charities to make a real difference, and it was great to learn about the different humanitarian approaches going on around the world during my master's.

When I'm planning my future career I don't give any thought to the fact that I'm in a wheelchair. I don't think this should stop me from working anywhere I want. Although I now work in an office the majority of the time I have no qualms about getting my hands dirty on site at the events the company I work for now, Tough Mudder, runs, and it has never been detrimental to my role that I can't walk or run up stairs (particularly as the team are now very used to picking me up whenever stairs get in the way!). This belief is echoed by the directors of the company I worked with alongside my master's, add-victor. They focus on placing ex-athletes and members of the armed forces into corporate internships and jobs regardless of any physical disability they may have.

There is a wheelchair marathon called the Outeniqua Challenge held in George on the Garden Route in South Africa every February. Alongside the elite marathon, the organizer, an incredible lady called Esther Watson, raised funds tirelessly to run an all-comers event for wheelchair users from around Southern Africa. In addition to entry into the fun run, 10 km race or marathon the people she invites are given transportation to George from as far as Zimbabwe, which takes three days on huge buses. They are also accommodated at the holiday park where the race starts and given free food and drink for the duration of the weekend. Attending this event showed me that my standards of what is wheelchair accessible and what is not really needed reassessing.

I initially entered the race because I'd heard that the prize money was good and the competition poor. I also wanted an excuse to leave the bleak weather in Britain to spend time with friends around Cape Town in the sunshine. The elite marathon has all the features you'd expect from what is marketed as a top-level international race: press conference the day before; athlete briefing with dodgy food;

media interviews at the start line. What I hadn't expected was the sheer number of wheelchair users registering alongside me for the different races and the poor state of their equipment. A lot of the participants in the fun run especially were pushing chairs that I wouldn't even consider using to get around my house. There were children in basketball chairs so big they could hardly reach the push-rims, old men in chairs with wooden wheels and nurses pushing men of my age who had lost limbs in some way or another through civil wars or bush witchcraft. Yet they manoeuvred around without a second thought, traversing the potholed ground and accepting the unequipped bathrooms without question. It was a humbling experience intensified by the athlete briefing in which the delight of all these participants to be given a bowl of pasta at the long tables filling the hall put to shame us elite athletes planning how to escape the event as soon as the speeches were over. I was really glad to have Mum there with me (she could never pass up an excuse to head back home!) when we went back to our five-star hotel where our every whim was taken care of. I felt so guilty that the feeling even outweighed my customary stomach-churning nerves the night before a marathon.

I was even more glad to have Mum there the next day after I won the race and was awarded my envelope of prize money. I casually left it on my lap and she immediately snatched it up and hid it away. A minute later I was surrounded by African athletes wanting to shake my hand and, if Mum was to be believed, to subtly relieve me of my prize. She practically dragged me away from my goodbyes to the other international athletes and back to our rental car. I hate to admit it but in this case her local knowledge, which I cruelly called 'racism', was pretty fortunate. Over the next few days I was inundated with messages on Facebook asking for money and equipment from people I hadn't even met who had been at the marathon, and one even accused me of promising to give her my racing chair. It isn't surprising, though. The amount of cash I had won would pay for ten participants to attend the event including accommodation, food and transport. That really put into perspective my own plans for the prize money, so with Esther's help I arranged to use it in a much more beneficial way, to fund athletes from other African countries to attend the race the next year. The Outeniqua Wheelchair Challenge is perhaps not the best marathon in the world, although at 28.1 miles as the 2011 race measured, it may be the best at that distance, but I hope that sponsors continue to support it in years to come for the sake of the great charity side of the event.

12

Around the World in Many Races

Without a doubt, having the opportunity to travel the world was the best bit of being an athlete. My friend Lou gave me a big wall map on which you can scratch off the gold layer over each country once you have visited it. I'm doing pretty well so far, although I need a trip to China or Russia to really make an impression on it! I've also added souvenirs from the places I've visited to the map so whenever I see it on my wall it brings back great memories. I always take hundreds of photos when I travel so spent hours during my gardening leave scrapbooking all my trips to give me a reminder of the great places I've been lucky enough to visit.

My love of travel is probably what got me through the horrible winter training in the rain with sub-zero temperatures day in, day out. Of course wanting to perform at my best in the summer races was a big enough incentive to work hard but in November, after a month of cold, hard training, March seems a long way away. When I had a race in a foreign country to look forward to I felt a lot happier during my training sessions. It might sound ridiculous but just hearing the starter's orders in an unfamiliar language or a foreign accent when I lined up for a race put me into a much more focused frame of mind. In race mode all my senses are heightened and I imagine the feeling of adrenaline is better than any synthetic high. That buzz is one of the biggest things I miss now I've given up racing.

I also miss some of the more comical moments that alleviated the pressure right before a race. At the England Athletics Championships they tried to disqualify all but one of the girls in my 800 m race as we weren't wearing club vests – unsurprising as none of us raced for a club, we all just had GB kit – and at a US meet the officials tried to remove the duct tape holding the seat of my chair in place. I'm not sure what performance advantage they thought a dirty bit of neon pink tape was going to give me but arguing is a pointless undertaking as officials tend to disqualify you if you annoy them! Thankfully the T53 women's class I raced in were quite a tightly knit bunch so we weren't too bothered by unusual happenings before our races. By the time you get to international level you're always racing the same girls and nine times out of ten you know the result of the sprints before they even start. There's always a buzz of nervous energy in the call room and when the competition isn't too serious a fair amount of banter, too. One 1500 m from 2011 in particular sticks in my mind – the US National Championships, to which international athletes are invited to compete. I didn't race the 1500 m normally but had entered for fun at the end of the meet and none of the other girls seemed to be taking it too seriously either. We gathered behind the start and when the starter called 'On your marks', we pulled forward in two rows as normal – when there are a large number of athletes racing a longer distance race we don't have to keep lanes. Then Amanda McGrory, one of the best middle-distance athletes in the world, suddenly screamed, 'Stop, there's a lizard!' A little green lizard had wandered onto the track and sat itself right between her back wheels almost underneath my front wheel. We all had to move so the starter could shift the lizard then start the whole process again, by which point we were giggling so much it's a wonder there were no false starts. Needless to say it wasn't the fastest race I've ever done! Normally, though, the banter on the start line is more around people trying to get an extra inch ahead or elbows clashing between lanes.

Lizards notwithstanding, once we'd been put in our lanes and everyone had stopped shuffling around and lining up wheels, the wait for the first starter's order was a tense one. My heart rate would shoot up so high that I felt like I was out of breath before the race even started and the nerves turned my arms to jelly. Then the call would come and we'd take our marks on the line. From this point my mind emptied of any nerves and everything was focused on listening for 'set', which was my signal to tense every muscle in my body like a coiled spring so I was ready to explode all my power into the first push when that gun went (although in my case my starts were always the weakest part of my race so it was never quite the explosion I was aiming for!). Everything would go quiet once the second order had been given and all I could hear was the blood pumping in my ears before the ear-splitting crack of the gun. When the gun sounded I didn't even have to think about making my arms move; they just went. Then my brain had to catch up and focus on getting the rest of the race done. My old coach Ian once said to his wife, the incredible Baroness Grey-Thompson, 'it's a good day to die' before she raced an important demo race at the Olympic Games. That's become a bit of a motto for all his athletes since, meaning we should leave everything we have on the track and push ourselves over what we think our limit is. When the lactic acid set in, especially during the 400 m, that motto always sprang to mind and made me force my burning, jelly-like arms to move harder, stronger and faster. There's nothing quite like the feeling of lactic acid. During the race it's not a sharp pain exactly; it's more like a debilitating feeling that spreads through your muscles gradually until as hard as you try they just won't contract. It sometimes even got to the point where I couldn't feel my forearms and was lit-erally going on muscle memory from the hours of training to push the wheels. Then the race finishes and it's like the worst cramp you've ever had setting in and making your arms feel like they are being torn off. It sounds crazy but that's why I love sport. The lung-burning, arm-cramping pain when I finish makes me want to train even though

I'm no longer racing thanks to the misplaced hope that if I train more the next session won't hurt quite so much. Of course that's never really the case; the harder you train the harder you can push yourself, so once the adrenaline's pumping any athlete, or even ex-athlete, won't feel like they've had a decent workout until that pain sets in.

There was a plus side to all the pain though – the celebrations when the meet was finished! For the first two years that I raced internationally I didn't see anything of the places I visited except the track or road course I was racing on, the hotel and the airport. If I was lucky I might also see inside a supermarket or restaurant but that was about it. I was working full-time so I had to be mindful of my limited holiday days, although LOCOG were very good about letting me take extra leave if necessary. I made a trip to Lisbon for the half marathon that lasted twenty-four hours, landing the night before the race and taking off two hours after I finished. In Berlin I was so determined to focus on the marathon that I didn't leave my hotel except to train and race for the four days I was there and came back with a very disdainful view of the city, not helped by the teeming rain and my double puncture during the race. Looking back, it was such a waste of visits to such beautiful cities.

Then I met Kyle and my racing trips became very different – and far better life experiences. We tried to actually get a taste of what the places we visited had to offer, however little that may have been in some cases. That didn't mean taking time off training, of course – we made sure to stick to our training programmes wherever we were in the world – but there were still plenty of hours left in the day for exploring, even when you factored in all the enforced rest before races. The destinations ranged from Windsor, Ontario, which at first glance seems to be the dullest concrete monstrosity of a university border town, to a revisit to Berlin, where we saw every sight in three days. In the past, on a trip to somewhere like Windsor I'd have ended up just chilling out at the hotel with all the other athletes for the duration of Boiling Point Track Classic, as even the event organizers advised us there was nothing to do there. Kyle was working at the track meet so we decided to wander down to the river that separates Canada from the USA and pushed for miles parallel to the sprawling greyness of Detroit, from which we could hear some sort of rock concert going on in the arena by the water on the US side. It was the perfect way to spend a boiling hot morning, and so much better than doing my training around a dusty track. All along the Windsor bank is a sculpture garden with amazing artwork of totally different styles. My favourite sat right by the barrier down to the water and featured an enormous iron elephant being trailed by a group of tiny baby ones with their trunks linked into each other's tails.

Once we reached the end of the sculpture garden we were confronted by temporary fencing forcing us away from the river, so we headed into the city for lunch at a cosy little sushi restaurant. While in the bathroom trying to fix my melted make-up I met a local girl who told me about a festival of local food, drink and live music starting that night down by the river, which explained the fenced-off section that had shepherded us back into the city centre. After lunch we headed back to the university where we were staying so that I could hit the track, then decided to visit the festival for dinner. Although I turned down some of the traditional Canadian food and drink, such as poutine, which is effectively chips with cheese curd and gravy, and a Caesar which is a Bloody Mary with extra clam juice (not the perfect drink the night before a track meet), the food was incredible. I didn't want a late night so we ate our cartons of hot chicken while listening to a local rock band as the sun went down then headed back along the river. As we strolled along it got darker and darker until all that was lighting our way was the glow from Detroit across the river and tiny pinpricks of light on the ground. At first I thought they were light bulbs put in the ground as a feature in the sculpture park but then I realized they were moving. They weren't light bulbs at all – they were fireflies! I'd never seen a firefly before so I'd never expected them to be quite so bright or to seemingly turn on and off by the second. I was like a little kid wanting to get closer to them so I could see each individual insect! Even without the fireflies I wouldn't have said Windsor was boring, however grey and ugly the city is, and after the added thrill of being escorted home by thousands of living light bulbs along the grass I'm even more glad I didn't stay in the hotel and play cards or watch movies with the other athletes. It really highlighted for me how much better my experience of racing could have been in the past. On top of that I achieved personal bests in the

100 m and 200 m at Boiling Point Track Classic so I have very happy memories of Windsor!

A few months later Kyle came over to Europe for the last few races of both our seasons, the Great North Run, Tunnel 2K and the Berlin Marathon. I had entered all of these at the start of the year when I was still trying to race both sprints and marathons so Ian and I discussed whether I should pull out of the Great North Run and Berlin. In the end we decided that I may as well race them as I had no more track meets that year and it would be good to see where I was. Tunnel 2K went fairly well for me but the Great North Run was a disaster for both of us, with Kyle crashing and me inexplicably pushing like a total novice and barely making it up the final hill. We both had the day off the next day and an easy week of training until we flew out to Berlin, so we decided while we were up in the north we would head off to Edinburgh to buy a kilt. I've spent a lot of time in the north of England but only popped up to the Scottish Borders once for a 10 km race, so I was keen to see more of Mum's family's country of origin. I found a hotel on the outskirts of Edinburgh in Leith that was right on the harbour and when we arrived they upgraded us to a water-view room that came complete with every pampering product you could ever want, as they saw we'd raced the Great North Run that morning. I could have spent all of the next day playing with the pedicure and manicure kits but, mindful of our mission to find the elusive kilt, we headed into the city and did our best to see every sight in Edinburgh and sample such traditional Scottish food as smoked salmon (me) and haggis (Kyle). The Edinburgh Dungeons evaded us due to health and safety regulations – only one wheelchair is allowed in the building at once – and we decided that experiencing them separately was a little pointless. We then tried to look around a gallery but that had steps up to the main floor and no lift. After a drive around to reach the bottom of the hill up to the Castle we assumed access up there would be just as bad as the rest of the city but actually it was a pleasant surprise. We were driven up to the Castle so we could avoid the long steep climb up the cobbles by a brilliant guide who told us all about the history of the roads and tunnels. But my favourite part was definitely getting to hold a sword and a gun that were hundreds of years old and insanely heavy to have had to fight with all day, and hearing the curator explain how many of our modern phrases and things we don't give a second thought about originated from the nuances of traditional weaponry. For example, men's shirts button up the opposite way to women's to prevent the hilt of the sword getting caught in the shirt edge when it was drawn from left to right by a right-handed swordsman (not, as I'd been told in the past, to make it easier for men to unbutton a woman's shirt while facing her!). The seven-hour drive home in the pouring rain was not so much fun as the day in Edinburgh had been but I'm so glad we took the detour as in one day we managed to cram in sightseeing that could have kept me occupied for a week.

And of course we found a kilt!

I'm very interested in languages and through listening

to athletes from other countries converse I've picked up
enough Swiss German and German to get by in those countries. It's proved very useful to have a grasp of German as
it's the one country I've been to where barely anyone seems
to speak English, and my role with Tough Mudder spans
Germany now so I'm relieved I have at least some grasp
of the language. When I punctured for the second time in
the 2010 Berlin Marathon I would have been totally stuck
if I hadn't been able to understand the directions from
where I was on the course back to my hotel. My grammar
is pretty nonexistent but thankfully the Germans are less
picky than the French so they gave me the chance to show
off my limited skills on our next stop on what became a bit
of a tour of European capital cities, Berlin. Embarrassingly
for someone who claims always to make the most of every
opportunity, I discovered on our first day in Berlin that the
hotel I had stayed in the year before, and that we were staying in again for this trip, was only a couple of streets away
from Checkpoint Charlie and the remains of the Berlin
Wall, yet I hadn't ventured outside the previous year. This
time round we made up for that. I like to try to immerse
myself in new places so I insisted we take the U-Bahn to
the marathon expo, where we had to go the day we arrived
to pick up our race numbers. It was only a short walk to
the station right beside Checkpoint Charlie so it gave us
a chance to take a look at the US guard re-enactment outside the (inaccessible) museum, which was pretty funny.
The train journey was a bit of an adventure as most of the
underground stations in Berlin are, like in London, old and

full of stairs, but eventually we found one on the map that had a lift and wasn't too far from the venue – and I even got to show off some of my German getting us there!

The expo itself was an impressive affair with the hangars at the old airport filled with stands representing every sports-related company you could think of either selling products or giving demos and information. Berlin is one of the only races I've done where the elite wheelchair athletes are not given their race numbers individually or at a special briefing, so it was quite a novelty getting to go to the expo and soak up the atmosphere surrounded by tens of thousands of runners who were preparing for the same race I was. Although the race was still over a day away it definitely brought on my nerves a little earlier than normal! The next day we used our training push to find the route from our hotel to the start of the race. Seeing all the stands and the start line we'd be lining up on the next day almost sent me over the edge. One thing I do wish I'd learned in the years I raced is to get a handle on the horrible pre-race nerves I experienced as I'm sure I'd have performed a lot better if I could sleep or eat before racing! Nevertheless those nerves definitely showed I was fully invested in the race. One of the biggest indicators to me that it was time to stop racing was the day I lined up on the start line with no nausea and realized that for the first time ever I didn't care if I won or lost.

Back in Berlin, I wanted to check out the finish area so I could see where to start sprinting, having never made it to the end of that particular marathon, so after lunch we went to watch the inline-skating marathon finish. It was one of the most impressive spectacles I've ever seen and I really think inline marathon should be an Olympic sport. The winner completed the course in just over an hour, which is much faster than even the wheelchair world record. It was incredible seeing the packs of athletes in their coloured lycra shoot past as fast as cyclists. Even better to watch were the slower participants rolling over the cobbles under the famous Brandenburg Gate, looking so exhausted but pleased to have reached the end, with women holding on to their partners and being partially pulled along in order for the pair to finish the race together. This seemed like a great idea to me considering my boyfriend was a marathon specialist and I was a sprinter . . .

'Check that out Kyle. It's so cute – that guy is pulling his wife along!'

'Haha! Poor guy. Pretty nice of him to wait for her.'

'I know. Guess they must really want photos together going under the gate! He must really love her . . .'

'Is that a hint?'

'Maaaaybe . . . You'd do that for me, right, babe?'

'Sure, if you can hit the men's A standard time for London qualification.'

So that was a no then! I raced pretty badly the next day thanks to a combination of having been training for sprints and using a new racing chair that did not fit at all. It was one of the toughest races I've done despite the flat course and as a result I missed the qualifying time for the Paralympic marathon in London. Rather than dwell on this, though, I was pretty pleased just to end what had been far too long a season since the first marathon in February. My much anticipated end-of-season light week meant that the next two days could be devoted to sightseeing and enjoying everything Berlin had to offer, starting with what we thought would be a scaled-down version of Cirque du Soleil. The Chamäleon theatre seemed like the perfect place to go to celebrate the end of the racing season as the seating was at tables where you could order drinks while watching the performance. As soon as it started we realized the show wasn't quite what we'd expected and I was pretty glad there was wine readily available to reduce any embarrassment due to having accidentally stumbled upon a cross between an acrobatics act and a strip club. It made for some interesting sights to say the least but I couldn't help laughing at the poor French couple at the table next to us trying to explain what was going on to their small children!

The best bit about finishing the season in Berlin was actually being able to have a night out without worrying that the next day I had to train or race. For most of the four years I raced my social life was constantly thwarted by athletics (although I also made a lot of friends and developed a whole new social life!). I missed countless birthday parties, reunions, nights out and girls' lunches thanks to having training sessions that clashed with arrangements or just needing to rest and live healthily. I was also travelling more than I was at home so the time I had to catch up with my friends from school and university was fairly limited. Having said that, summers with Tough Mudder are pretty similar on the travel front, but at least there's always time for a party while we're away! At one UK Athletics psychology seminar the psychologist asked us about things we monitor and when I started talking about training he stopped me and said that my training didn't seem to be a problem – what I needed to work on was having a social life! Although I'm sure he was joking, that throwaway comment annoyed me a lot. I love to travel to see new sights and meet new people and what's great about travelling with athletics is getting to experience different countries with friends from around the world.

In 2011 my birthday fell on the same day as the Oensingen Marathon in Switzerland, which would probably have been a disappointment for most people but I was actually really excited. Yes, I had to race a 42 km Paralympic qualifier the evening of my birthday but it meant that afterwards all my athletics friends from as far as Australia and New Zealand would be in one place to celebrate with me. As soon as the marathon was over the athletes who had only raced the 14 km course were on hand to start the celebrations and, as I hadn't exactly kept it quiet that it was my birthday, the staff at the post-race dinner gave us as much chocolate cake as we could eat. Once the bus finally dropped us back at the SPZ in Nottwil it felt like being back at university again, getting ready for a night out. My coach had rented a house the other side of the village where I was supposed to be staying but rather than go back there Aussie hospitality ruled and we all got ready in their team corridor like when I was living in halls. It's a pretty good testament to Swiss quality that the electricity didn't blow with the number of hairdryers and straighteners being used on that floor! Nottwil is the tiniest town with nothing of interest in it aside from the Swiss Paraplegic Centre. However, it does have a 'beach village' with a surf shop and bar down beside the lake so I celebrated turning twenty-three at the beach with about forty of my friends from all around the world. There were Aussies, Americans, Canadians, Swiss, Germans and Italians but, hilariously, not a single Brit aside from myself. So when a psychologist accuses me of replacing friends with athletics I don't think they quite understand the circuit we race on! Through athletics I've met more people than I even did working as a shot girl at university so now I can travel the world and know that wherever I go I'll have friends to have fun with.

13

Getting Around

Travelling on the Tube around London is very different when you're in a wheelchair. Not only do I actually have to plan new journeys online before I go to avoid unexpected steps but also people talk to me during the journey! In the seven years I used the London Underground before I broke my back I probably spoke to two strangers. Now people approach me on almost every journey. I'm not sure what it is about being in a wheelchair that makes me more approachable but it certainly seems to have made a big difference. I've lost count of how many times people have stood in front of me to protect me from the crush of commuters and made comments along the lines of 'this must be even worse for you than for the rest of us'. Actually, no it isn't – I'm guaranteed a seat every time I travel, even on the commuter trains into the City! It is a little annoying when people don't give up the disabled area by the door of the carriage, though, as people don't see me so I get a lot of bottoms in my face, which isn't pleasant. It's also dangerous for everyone else as they can't reach the pole to hold on to with me in the way and they trip over my wheels.

At 7 a.m. when I'm already exhausted from a morning workout and the tolls of a job with really long hours I'm not the most sociable of people but strangely I've met some really great people on the early morning tube. On my journeys into Canary Wharf when I worked at LOCOG, an ex-military man named Harvey would get on the same carriage as me and wait patiently for the station assistant to give me a hand up the foot-high step onto the Metropolitan line tube. Then one morning the assistant was busy so Harvey put down his briefcase and gave me a push. For a few weeks he did this every morning and we got chatting. I was reading E. H. Gombrich's *A Little History of the World*, partially in a bid to fill in some of the gaping holes in my knowledge of world history but mainly to appear intellectual, and we got chatting about books. The next day he brought Jo Nesbø's Norwegian crime novel *The Snowman* for me to borrow and that started a six-month-long book swap! It's amazing how many great people in the past I might have spent hours a day within ten feet of and never said a word to. Now I'm in a wheelchair some of those people actually approach me so I've made lots of new acquaintances from all walks of life.

I do occasionally need a hand up the bigger steps onto and off the carriages so it's nice when people offer to help before I ask. I hate arriving at a station and seeing a huge step up to the platform when the doors open, then having to shout at commuters so they can hear me asking for a push over their iPods. Every night coming home from Canary Wharf I'd go through the same frustrating rigmarole of not being able to get off the Jubilee line at Finchley Road to change onto the Metropolitan line without a kind person taking pity on me rather than just shoving past me and swearing at me for being in the way (oh yes, it happened many, many times). That's one of the great things about my new commute into the City – I can do the whole journey with no help!

As much as I understand that many of the stations are very old, so putting lifts in them is unaffordable, it does feel frustrating that I can travel the world on my own and never have to ask for help, yet I can't get closer to Covent Garden or Leicester Square by Tube than Westminster! I guess I'm lucky to be young and fit enough that I can get around the London Underground using escalators and brute strength to push myself up steep slopes and pull myself up steps onto trains. It doesn't always go to plan though. One particularly memorable night I slipped trying to pull myself off the tube onto a raised platform by digging my fingers into the ridges at the edge of the concrete (yes, recipe for disaster!) and pitched headfirst out of my chair, dropping all my belongings under the train. What made it fifty times worse was that all the people in the carriage that my now empty wheelchair was rolling around in just watched and didn't even think to pass my wheelchair onto the platform. Luckily Transport for London have long grabbing devices at stations so they can pick rubbish (and in this case my belongings) up off the track so I didn't have to lean down and risk having my head taken off by the next tube. With the way my luck was going that day that would have been the likely outcome of any trackside acrobatics! I've also learned the hard way why the station attendants always try to stop me from riding the escalators to get in and out of the underground tunnels. It's very simple to go up and down an escalator in a wheelchair just by holding onto the moving handrails. As two of my Australian friends demonstrated, you can even manage it in a pair side by side if you hold on to each other. What isn't so easy, however, is riding an escalator with no hands, as a commuter in a very big rush to get home from Canary Wharf taught me one night after work. He ran down the escalator and pushed my arm out of the way to get past, sending me tumbling backwards. It was pretty scary but if I'm honest mainly just embarrassing as I'd assured the people getting on after me that I didn't need any help. Fortunately the woman behind caught me before I got to the bottom of the flight and dragged me out of the way of the teeth that swallow the steps so only my hair got tangled in them, and someone else rescued my wheelchair and helped me back in. I had a lump on my head for days after that one but as the lifts were broken for months on end at Canary Wharf station during the time I worked at LOCOG I was back riding that escalator the next morning. It's a trick that always gets attention but I'm keeping my fingers crossed I never cause people to stare out of horror as I clatter down again!

It's not just when I'm travelling that being in a wheelchair seems to draw people's attention. A few years after my accident we made a family trip to Devon for my nana's eightieth birthday lunch along with other members of my dad's extended family from all over England. I had brought along a copy of the London 2012 Paralympic photography book *Power and Movement* in which I'm featured to show her and she was thrilled and surprised when she opened it at the gorgeous Michelin-starred restaurant on the seafront where we were celebrating. When it came to dessert time I declined and so was very confused when a flaming tower was placed in front of me with a little gold cylinder beside it. It turned out that the chef had been asked to cook an Olympic-themed dessert for the Team GB and Paralympics GB fundraising event at the Royal Albert Hall in 2012 so when the waiter saw the book lying on the table they decided to test out the Olympic flame and medal dessert combination on me. I have to admit it didn't take much to distract me from my unhealthy food abstinence and savour every last mouthful!

Back at the hotel the whole family gathered for tea and more present-opening for Nana. My sister and I needed a break so we left the tea room overlooking the bay and walked through the bar to get to the bathrooms. She couldn't believe how people stopped mid-sentence just to stare at my wheelchair. I'd changed out of the mini I'd worn for lunch into a very boring jeans and blazer combination but still people looked at me like I was something from another planet. I've become pretty used to strangers losing any ounce of the tact they'd pay to an able-bodied person who looked a bit unusual so I either ignore the stares or smile brazenly back. Fi, however, was slightly less subtle. She looked disdainfully around the room at all the swivelled heads and proclaimed at the top of her voice, 'God it's like you're some sort of national attraction.' The heads turned away pretty fast. Ironically, later that evening Fi and I walked down to the seafront to find food and it was her, being tall, skinny and stunning with waist-length hair and perfect natural style, who was getting stared at and wolf-whistled by every guy we passed!

It seems like there's some sort of complication or comedy happening at least half the time I travel on public or commercial transport, especially in the UK. I'd much rather drive a journey than take on planes, trains or buses, as at least then I know I'm going to get to my destination, but unfortunately if I drove into London I'd be late to every appointment so I'm a pretty regular sight jumping on and off tubes and buses. London buses are especially frustrating as they only allow one wheelchair on at a time, so when I'm playing tour guide for visiting athletes that method of transport becomes out of the question. The Tube stations in central London are also mainly inaccessible so I've become pretty adept at finding shortcuts between the main sights so we can push from place to place. I've lost count of the number of times buses have stopped to pick up passengers where I'm waiting and driven off when they saw me in a wheelchair even after I've pressed the ramp request button. This happened one time when I was with an able-bodied friend who had already boarded the bus; he tried to stop the driver and was told my wheelchair would be in the way of the pram space. I don't even know what to say to that ridiculous explanation for laziness. Getting the ramp out takes one push of a button and adds a few extra seconds to the other passengers' journeys. Leaving me behind adds at least twenty minutes to mine and is also illegal. Not a difficult choice, or so you'd think.

If I am lucky enough to make it onto public transport, avoiding the usual complications of drivers not wanting to pick me up, broken lifts and step-free access only applying to one platform at a station I've expected to change at, once I get on the bus or train I seem to be catnip for lunatics, as well as the lovely people I've met. When I was commuting to LOCOG in Canary Wharf I had to get a later tube than the one I wanted every morning to avoid a very sweet but not quite all there man who told me all about his life every day while we waited on the platform then sat on my wheel for the duration of his tube ride with his plastic bag of belongings resting on my leg. Even on the other side of the world in Sydney I was chatting with my boyfriend on the train from Olympic Park to the city one morning when an extremely drunken lady came up to me and started rubbing the sun block I'd missed into my back. I wasn't quite sure what to do so just smiled, thanked her and hoped I hadn't missed any elsewhere! The encounters I find the strangest, though, are those where people talk to me as though I'm incapable of being independent just because I'm in a wheelchair, despite the fact I've obviously made it onto the same tube as them. On my way to a meeting in London a man was talking to the station attendant, while I waited at the platform, about the most expensive stamp in the world and how he was travelling to see it when it came to Amersham. When the train arrived he got in my carriage, sat across the aisle from me, and started telling me I should come with him to see it to 'get me out of the house'. Well as I don't live on a Metropolitan line train from Chorleywood to Finchley Road I think it was pretty safe to say I was out of the house and therefore not in need of a trip to the stamp fair. I do meet some great people on the tube, though, too, like Harvey and other nice commuters who help to shield me from the worst of the rush-hour crush. Believe me, if you think it's bad being rammed into a stranger at head height, imagine how bad it is when your head is at groin level.

Aeroplane travel can be even worse than public transport as the airlines have more freedom to make up their own rules rather than having to make sure they are accessible to everyone. As soon as they say a seemingly discriminatory rule is for health and safety reasons nobody dares argue with them. On a flight to Miami with a fellow athlete who is also a wheelchair user, on our way to race the US National Championships, there was an unexplained delay at the gate before we began taxiing for take-off. We waited and waited and finally a manager from the land side approached him and I, and asked where our carers were. We were a little confused and said we were travelling alone, at which point we were told it was airline policy not to let wheelchair users fly without an able-bodied companion.

We voiced our disbelief and were further insulted to be told we needed to have a carer in case the plane crashed as we wouldn't be able to get ourselves to the exit. Now I understand that in some cases this would be true but the staff had watched him and I jump on and off the seats and climb over the armrests they couldn't figure out how to move so it was obvious we were mobile. In fact, we'd probably get ourselves to the exit faster than a lot of the able-bodied passengers. After a further long delay they gave in and let us travel purely because they didn't want to delay the flight any longer to get our bags off. Needless to say I won't be travelling with that airline again! We were lucky the staff didn't spot our travelling arrangements when we checked our baggage though. When the US Paralympic team were travelling to a major championships they were told every wheelchair user needed a carer or none of the group could travel. Unlike the Great Britain team the Americans have a lot of wheelchair users so there were not enough staff members to go around to take the place of carers. Their amputee and walking cerebral palsy athletes ended up having to act as carers despite the fact that some of them were less able to move than the people they were supposedly caring for. That's the stigma of a wheelchair I suppose – uninformed policy writers assume that anyone who sits down in a chair is an incapacitated body yet as soon as someone can walk they are considered able however slow and unbalanced that walking actually is.

I admit that sometimes my expectations of what I can and can't do are a little high but I would much rather be given the chance to try to do something independently than be told I'm incapable by someone who knows my abilities far less well than I do. On a flight to Switzerland last year I had the choice of going up wet metal stairs on my bum as the platform lift was broken, being carried by the ground staff, or delaying the plane to wait for another lift. I chose to climb up on my bum as I trust my own arms more than those of people I've never met to get me up a flight of slippery stairs. Climbing took only a couple of minutes and then I had to wait at the top of the stairs for someone to carry my chair up. During this time I wrote a jokey message to Tanni on Twitter about it with a photo of the stairs, and by the time I'd made it to my seat on the plane I had over twenty new followers, all of whom were telling me in various ways to sue the airport. Most of these people were disabled. To me it's far worse that these people are so reliant on having the perfect service there for them that they think it's worth suing a company over a mechanical failure that wasn't their fault, rather than occasionally sliding around the floor on your bum. On the way back to the UK, as there was no aisle chair ready at the gate to get me off the plane, I'd have had to wait forty minutes for assistance and delayed the cabin crew's trips home so again I just bum shuffled down the aisle. I really appreciated the way the staff handled my slightly unorthodox methods of movement. They offered once to help, I said no, and they let me get on with it. Having spent so many years travelling alone or with family or team-mates who are familiar with the rigmarole of air travel in a wheelchair it's been pretty funny seeing the reactions of my co-workers at add-victor and Tough Mudder to the preferential treatment I receive at the airport and the bizarre treatment that starts once I begin trying to board. Everyone's always pleased to be allowed to skip the lines, and I've also been pleasantly surprised by how great they are about dealing with the inevitable delays caused by no aisle chairs being available to get me off the plane or a lack of staff allowed to push them. In one case our Operations Director calmly picked me up and carried me off a plane back from Germany to save waiting an hour for assistance, and since then he's also piggybacked me on and off buses and into hotels too. I guess that's the bonus of working with someone who's also carried you around a large proportion of a 12-mile muddy obstacle course!

14

Great Britain

My first selection to the Great Britain athletics team came before the International Wheelchair and Amputee Sports Federation U23 World Championships in 2010. I had qualified for the U23 World Championships in 2009 as well but unsurprisingly had not been selected as I hadn't even been wheelchair racing for a year and did not have the experience required to represent my country. I was therefore very nervous about 2010 selection as it would be my last chance to race internationally as an Under-23 athlete. At the time I was in the midst of filming a documentary with Channel 4 so the producers had found out from UK Athletics when they would be calling me to tell me if I'd been selected. This meant that not only did I have my usual manic day of training and work at LOCOG to contend with, but also had to deal with having a film crew following me from the moment I woke up, through my daily commute and around the office. It would have been a stressful enough day without waiting to hear whether I'd finally get the chance to wear that famous red, white and blue lycra for the first time!

The morning passed in a blur of licensed product approvals, and I'm pretty sure I must have approved hundreds of incorrect London 2012 logo applications and wonky pictograms. Every few seconds I would surreptitiously check my phone to make sure I hadn't missed any calls from Birmingham, where the UK Athletics Head Office was based at that time. Finally a little after lunch it rang. The film crew gathered around my desk and everyone in the Licensing and Retail team stopped what they were doing to listen to my side of the call. Thankfully it was good news! I'd been selected to race the T53 100 m, 200 m, 400 m and 800 m, and on top of that to race as a T54 in the 1500 m and 5000 m. It was better than I ever could have expected. I'm one of those people who cries more at good news than bad so I was desperate to escape the group of people surrounding me and head to the bathroom before I started crying in the office. Unfortunately, Channel 4 had other ideas. They made the whole office cheer for what was one of the most embarrassing few minutes of my life. Then they made them repeat the ordeal for take after take. Until that point I'd been fairly unbothered by having a film crew filming every important moment in my life for two years but that day they really annoyed me.

Representing Great Britain is an honour I'd never even dreamed of before I broke my back. Although my family is scattered around the world and I have ties to many countries, I always felt completely British. I had a giant flag on my wall at my parents' house and even my suitcase is printed with the Union Jack! The day my big box of red, white and blue adidas warm-up and competition kit arrived and I tried on the Union-Jack-printed crop top and blue leggings completely made up for not being able to walk. This time I told the film crew to leave me alone to celebrate with my family, and I think my parents were even prouder than they were when I found out I'd been accepted to Oxford University. I couldn't wait to get to Olomouc in the Czech Republic where the U23 World Championships were taking place and start racing for my country.

Early on Thursday, 19 August 2010 the Great Britain U23 team met at London Heathrow to fly to Prague from where we'd travel by coach for three hours to get to Olomouc, a small town in the east of the Czech Republic. The team included disabled runners, throwers and jumpers in addition to the three wheelchair racers. From the moment we all congregated in the check-in area I felt totally at home among the athletes, many of whom had been competing for years longer than me. I was really pleased that among them were Jonnie Peacock and Scott Moorhouse, who started competitive athletics through the British Paralympic Association Fast Track Power and Performance Programme in 2009 with me. The atmosphere was fantastic and it reminded me of just how much I'd missed being part of a team since I'd stopped playing lacrosse when I became a wheelchair user.

We got onto the plane without any mishap and the flight went by in a flash of giggling and chatting. When we landed in Prague there was no aisle chair for me or one of the guys on the team who also has paralysed legs, so I had to shuffle down the aisle on my bum to get to the enormous wheelchairs they had waiting for us at the terminal. Ordinarily I would refuse to get into the airport chairs that have to be pushed by attendants but as there were two of us going through the embarrassment it didn't seem so bad, and it wasn't long before we were reunited with our own well-fitted everyday chairs. The amount of equipment we had as a team was pretty substantial and I'm very impressed that every throwing frame, racing wheelchair and javelin made it onto the tiny carousel at Prague airport to be grabbed by the swarm of UK Athletics staff who took complete control of all our travel arrangements. Next up, the coach to Olomouc. We were sharing transport with athletes from Iraq and the United Arab Emirates, who had already boarded the coach by the time we got our towers of baggage together and made it out of the terminal. It was pretty clear that some of the Iraqi team members were less than enamoured with Great Britain and would not be moving from the accessible seating downstairs to allow those of us without use of our legs to find a seat. Never mind, a bit of climbing would provide good footage for Channel 4's documentary so we got out the Handycam they'd lent me and I bum shuffled up to a table while my friends Jade, Scott and Joe filmed (and mocked) me. I couldn't believe how fast the journey went. It was like being on the coach for a school trip, playing cards and singing kids' songs, and I'm pretty sure I regressed at least ten years for the duration of the trip!

The access didn't get a whole lot better once we made it to the hotel. The breakfast and meeting areas were up a small flight of marble stairs which had the world's slowest platform lift which could only take one of the many international athletes that needed to use it at a time. I took one look at the queue of wheelchair users waiting their turn at breakfast time on the morning after we arrived and decided my stomach couldn't wait that long. I climbed the stairs on my bum again while one of our throwers carried my chair up. In hindsight this might have been a time to remember the old saying 'patience is a virtue'. If that's the case then I'm not a very virtuous person and it cost me in a big way at that competition. The day before the competition started I was climbing the stairs to get to our team meeting and my bum slipped off the marble step. I fell, jerking my shoulder hard. For the rest of the trip it was agony and had to be taped up with neon-pink Kinesio tape. I couldn't even push my everyday chair let alone my race chair without pain. I'd been expected to win at least three gold medals and two silvers but with the state of my shoulder I only managed a silver and three bronze medals and didn't even finish the 5000 m. I was absolutely gutted.

I can't blame my poor performance entirely on my sore shoulder, which turned out to be caused by a grade two tear to my infraspinatus that plagued the rest of my season and prevented me from qualifying for the marathon at the senior World Championships. My first race at the U23 World Championships was the 100 m and the admittedly small stands were completely packed with spectators of all different nationalities waving flags of more countries than I could recognize. As we lined up for the gun I felt as though an iron fist was compressing my chest and I started to panic that I would let the Great Britain team down. My brain went to mush and I couldn't even remember how to start, let alone react to the gun. By the time I reached the 20 m mark some of the other girls were nearing the half way point. Inside I was screaming at my arms to move faster but I couldn't get them to coordinate. My start has always been the weakest part of my race so I caught up to and overtook some of the other athletes in the finishing metres, but I still finished in fourth place, out of the medals. There's a saying in athletics that if you come fourth you may as well come last as nobody will remember it and unfortunately it's true. With their usual fabulous timing Channel 4 appeared before I'd even cooled down and thrust a camera in my face, asking how the race had gone. My reply was unprintable and I pushed away as fast as I could into the woods that ran alongside the track complex. It didn't take long for Jade to finish her race, winning her first of many gold medals, and find me sobbing in a dark area just off the path. We'd become close through sharing Ian as a coach and rooming together at various track meets around Europe, including the U23 World Championships, the past two summers so it was great to have her there as she understood exactly how bad I felt. After a few minutes I regained my composure and we pushed slowly around the woods and back to the track to find Ian for a post-race debrief.

Ian was a great coach for me as he tempered the

overreactions I was prone to after every race. He was slow to praise but only reprimanded in a jokey or constructive way, so when he was watching I was even more desperate to perform well to try to get a 'that was all right' or even a 'good' out of him. 'Good' only happened once when I knocked an hour off my London Marathon time in a year, though! If a race doesn't go as planned I suffered a lot with confidence and when I don't have a coach there to put it into perspective one bad race at the start of the competition could write off all the distances I still had left to race. If a race went well I could become over excited and distracted, which was also bad news for any further races as I needed to be able to get back into race mode sometimes within half an hour of finishing the previous race. The first thing Ian always asked was, 'How did that feel?' It might sound silly but just those four words from him were enough to calm me down. They'd make me evaluate each stage of the race until I could take something good from the worst race, even if that was merely a lesson to be learned or something to be improved on, and I realized that even the best performance had its flaws that needed to be ironed out in the next race. I'm very glad he was able to come to Olomouc for the first few days of competition. He was not the team coach so he made the long drive from the north of England just to support Jade and I. Needless to say that made me even more determined not to mess up the rest of my races.

After that first disaster of a 100 m my performance improved and I medalled in the remainder of my races.

Not the golds I'd been hoping for, but with the searing pain in my shoulder I guess I was lucky to make it onto the podium at all. I don't think I'll ever quite get over not getting to hear that national anthem and have the British flag raised for me, though! The medals ceremonies provided a lot of amusement for our rather excitable team. The majority of them took place in the pouring rain so the British athletes looked for any excuse to miss them in favour of relaxing at the hotel after a hard day's racing. However, we all stayed behind (in the sunshine for once) to watch Joe Allen be presented with the 5000 m gold medal he'd beaten an Iraqi athlete to. He was another new athlete to the Great Britain team so it was a great achievement. As the Union Jack was raised and the first bars of 'God Save The Queen' rang out, the Iraqi stepped off the podium and tried to walk away. He was stopped by the Czech officials who had presented the medals and was pushed back onto the podium. He immediately stepped back off. It turned into a strange scene like something out of a bad aerobics video with this young athlete stepping on and off the block until finally the anthem ended and he could walk away in peace. After the competition was over and we were free to celebrate we found out why he'd behaved so bizarrely. His brother had been killed by coalition forces in the Iraq war a few years before, during an attack in which he lost his arm. Until then the war had always felt like something that didn't involve me and I've never felt it was my place to take sides as to whether it should have happened, but it really brought it home seeing how another athlete had been affected by it and how much he hated all British and American people as a result.

Although I didn't perform quite as well as I'd hoped to at the U23 World Championships I was hopeful of selection to the UK Athletics development squad for 2010. I was already a member of the training academy so making the funded squad was my next goal. Unfortunately, I was not successful, which was disappointing but not a huge surprise having been racing for less than two seasons. A year later, though, after a successful 2011 season in which I raced personal bests in all the T53 track distances from 100 m to 800 m and achieved the International Paralympic Committee A qualifying standards for London 2012 across all those distances, putting me into the top ten in world senior rankings, I was a lot more confident that I would be selected for the UK Athletics development squad. This time I found out via a post on another athlete's Facebook wall that once again I'd been overlooked. It would be fair to say I was quite confused and hurt by the decision to leave me out of the squad, but it pushed me to train even harder to prove that I did deserve to be selected.

My desire to be a member of the UK Athletics squad had nothing to do with wanting the funding. Sure, it would have been amazing to be able to stay in the nice hotels that the team were put up in and to be able to have physio and massage as often as I needed it rather than as often as I could afford it, but at the end of the day as long as I had a bed in which to get some rest before competition day it made little difference to me whether that bed was in a five-star hotel or in a basic guest house or motel. What I hated about not being on the squad, yet being invited to the same international races as the members of the Great Britain squad, was not being a part of the team camaraderie that I experienced in Olomouc in 2010. As a result though I met lots of athletes from other nations, which gave me the opportunity to train with Madison de Rozario, one of the top T53 girls in the world in Australia, and with Keira Frie, a top T54 racer, in Canada, now two of my close friends. This couldn't have been a bad thing for my performance as I'm sure these girls must be doing something right, so any tips I could pick up were golden. It was also great to train with friends whom I wasn't in competition with for squad spaces as it took the edge off the constant pressure we are under to perform for a place on the team. We were just friends who happened to all be interested in athletics. Sharing rooms and apartments with international athletes definitely added to the fun on racing trips, too. In Canberra I was put in an apartment with seven Canadian men. I have no problem rooming with guys and at least I had met all of the Canadians, which is sometimes not the case when you are allocated rooms. The afternoon we arrived I went to freshen up in the bathroom after the long coach ride from Sydney and locked the door behind me. Next thing I knew the door opened and Curtis Thom, a friend of mine on the Canadian team, wheeled right in. Cue much laughter (from the guys) and mild panic (from me) as we realized the lock on the door was broken. Seeing professional athletes naked might sound like a good thing but it's not an arrangement I'd rush to repeat! Nevertheless despite the ups and downs of international flights and room allocations the excitement of travelling to a race or training camp is something I really miss. Although I still get to fly to Europe with my job now the travel is definitely not something I get excited about (except when I'm going out to our HQ in New York) – it generally just means I'll be knackered for the rest of the week which is not something to look forward to. I still love the time abroad once I get there though, whether it's for meetings or for an event, so I'm very glad I didn't end up with a job that meant no travel at all!

15

Back to Real Life

As much as not getting selected for the London Paralympics was a disappointment, the Summer of 2012 was one of the best of my life. As soon as I saw the team list (without my name on it of course) I booked a flight to Canada and flew out immediately to spend two weeks road tripping with my boyfriend Kyle from Saskatoon to Clearwater via Edmonton, Jasper, Radium Springs, Calgary and a gorgeous vineyard in British Columbia (where I was very glad I'd wheeled my way out of driving duty!). It was difficult to feel any regret that I hadn't made the team while driving through the looming Rockies, kayaking across picture-perfect lakes and climbing mountains to see breathtaking views of crashing waterfalls. It was the first summer since 2007 either of us had had a holiday rather than spending it racing or working so we were determined to make the most of it – and I was particularly determined to see a bear whilst we were camping! Aside from the mosquitos and the retch-inducing environment of wilderness bathrooms a trip into Canadian back-country was exactly what I needed to step back and figure out where my life was going before heading back to the craziness of London as an Olympic city.

As an athlete, an ex-LOCOG employee and, most importantly of all, a Londoner it's difficult to describe how it felt being in the front row for so much Olympic and Paralympic action. I've been lucky enough to attend countless rugby matches to cheer on the Wasps and England, but until the London Olympics I'd never really watched other sport live. I was always on the other side of the barriers, so immersed in the races I was taking part in that I never took a breath and savoured the atmosphere that an international competition brings.

The Olympic ticket ballot definitely worked out in my favour and I was pretty shocked when I found out I'd been allocated tickets to every day of the Olympic cycling, including the road race and time trial, and the men's coxless IV final of the rowing. One of the big upsides of not being selected to race the Paralympics was that I could actually use my Olympic tickets rather than being away on holding camp with the GB Paralympians.

I'd seen the inside of the Olympic Park many times on tours with clients during its construction and had even raced in the Stadium at the Paralympic Athletics test event, but entering the Park for my first event as a spectator was incredible. Seeing all the products I'd worked on in the merchandise stores and the branding I'd become so used to applying to apparel on enormous boards and banners made me really appreciate how incredible an opportunity working at LOCOG was. I may not have been making a difference in the charitable sense of the word, but it was pretty cool that my decisions had even a small effect on what so many people around the world purchasing Olympic memorabilia now have in their homes. With that and the whirlwind of medals our talented athletes won it made for a very memorable two weeks!

Even the weeks between the Olympic and Paralympic Games were special. After a holiday with my mum and sister I returned to carry the Paralympic flame in the torch relay as part of the WheelPower team. I'm the first to admit that until I arrived at Stoke Mandeville Stadium, from where I'd be carrying the torch, I never really understood the appeal or the significance of the flame. Then I met the daughter of Sir Ludwig Guttman (founder of the Paralympic Games) daughter and it hit home. It was such an honour to be part of a team that also included a descendant of someone whose work had had such a profound impact on my ability to live like a 'normal' person, despite over half of my body being paralysed. When the time came for the torch to be handed to me it took a lot of effort not to let the tears escape, particularly with my friends, family and Kyle all there to watch. Then the next day my Paralympic experience got even better. A friend I worked with at LOCOG called to say she had a spare ticket to the Paralympic Opening Ceremony, and would I like to go? Kyle had just flown in to see the torch relay and we had planned to watch the Ceremony on TV like most of the world, so I had to say no. A few hours later another call came – she'd found a second ticket so Kyle and I could both see the incredible spectacle live. We quickly jumped on the tube and made it to the Park in time for a reunion dinner with my old LOCOG team, before taking our seats for what turned out to be an incredibly emotional evening. The Ceremony was amazing, and seeing my friend Joe zipline in and light the torch, then watching so many of my friends from around the world take part in the athletes' parade made me very proud (and I'll admit, a little jealous!).

In addition I had tickets to Paralympic rowing, tennis and every day of the Paralympic athletics thanks to friends and family buying tickets in the hope I'd be racing, and friends competing in the other sports giving me spectator tickets. Heading back to the Park the next day I was a bit nervous that I'd feel that same pang of jealousy watching my friends race in the Stadium. Strangely though, once we got there I was just happy to see all the other classes race and cheer on my friends, without having any desire to be out on the track. The only exception to this was when the results to the races I'd qualified for came up. Even without hitting my PBs I could see that I'd have made the top five in the finals so the frustration became pretty intense. I think that probably showed me that it was time to have a real think about whether or not I should continue to race in athletics. If the only thing that made me want to be on the track was indignation that I could have beaten some of the girls who were selected for other nations, and that there was no GB representation in my races, rather than having the desire to be out on the track for the love of the sport then I obviously wasn't racing for the right reasons anymore. As much as sport was my job for four years it's still just sport and therefore it should still have been fun. By the time it got to the Paralympic marathon, which I went to watch with a friend on the US track team, I'd decided it was time for me to hang up my lycra. Then the marathon brought back the doubts – and the jealousy. It's hard to describe how much I wanted to be lined up on that start line. Every time the athletes passed us on their laps this feeling grew until the adrenaline rush I felt cheering on Shelly Woods as she sprinted to the finish line left me as exhausted as if I'd been racing too.

As Rio 2016 had always been a more realistic goal for me than London 2012, I'd never intended to stop racing if I wasn't selected, but the plan had been to deprioritise sport for a year whilst moving into paratriathlon, a new sport for the Rio Games, and do a master's while working part-time to supplement my SportsAid funding and Loughborough scholarship. After the emotional rollercoaster of spectating at the Paralympics though I refined that a bit – I'd just race a few road races on top of the triathlon training to keep my head in 'professional athlete mode'. I'd assumed that the hardest thing with taking up triathlon would be fitting it in around university and work, but in reality, compared to the time-management skills I'd needed to get through my Oxford undergrad, the time pressure was no issue at all. What I hadn't factored in was the toll adding in swimming and cycling to my training would take on my body. The shoulder I injured at U23 World Championships never really recovered fully due to the continued strain I put on it with training to make the London team while I was still supposed to be rehabilitating it, and it didn't take long for lifting my left arm above my head to swim freestyle to become excruciatingly painful. Then the pain started on the bike too, so I ended up cycling with one arm doing all the work. I decided this meant I should just train more in my chair rather than actually letting my tendons heal, and entered Padova Marathon in April 2013. It was a horrible wet race only brightened up by my mum and sister coming out to Italy to watch me and ply me with ice cream and pizza afterwards. By the time I finished one hand was pouring with blood from the sharp edge of my glove which had snapped in half and I couldn't move the wrist on my other arm thanks to what turned out to be an inflamed tendon, and of course my shoulder was agony.

Despite the top-class coaching and sports medicine support my TASS Scholarship at Loughborough gave me, neither my shoulder or my wrist healed in the six weeks they suggested I lower the intensity of my training for. In hindsight (and now that my shoulder still permanently hurts) I should have taken the time off to rest, but once again I was desperate just to do one more race and entered the Great Manchester Run without getting a single training session in during the six weeks between Padova and that race. I won it, but it was a painful and undeserved win as I knew I was not the best athlete on the day, I just had the best tactics. Sitting on the makeshift podium hearing the National Anthem and feeling like I didn't deserve the medal around my neck was not a feeling I ever want to repeat, but it finally made me realize that it was time to stop. When I got back to Loughborough I booked in for an operation to alleviate the pain in my shoulder and called it quits with elite sport.

After giving up training I had so much more time on my hands around classes that I decided to move back to London and work more hours at add-victor. The team there are so incredible that it didn't even feel like work showing up to the office every day, and I really believe in the work they're doing to teach big businesses that the transferable skills athletes and ex-armed forces officers have are worth so much more than certificates from any university when it comes to actually being effective in the workplace. It was a very hard decision to leave when Tough Mudder offered me the job running their European Partnerships, but to turn down the opportunity to work with such a young and fast-growing company with so many in-built opportunities for me to develop my business knowledge would have been the wrong decision in the long-term. After training at Tough Mudder HQ in New York I returned to London to take on the challenge of signing up sponsors for our European events, making sure everything goes smoothly for those sponsors on site and working with our Retail Manager in the US to execute our European licensed merchandise range. My role is pretty varied and with so much to do to put on all our events and make our Mudders happy, and such a small EMEA office to do it all, I get to work really closely with our Innovations and Operations teams. It's great seeing what they do and incorporating their goals into what I'm working with sponsors on, as with LOCOG being so big I didn't really have much contact with the teams on the ground outside our Commercial Negotiations department.

Of course being part of such a dynamic company and being lucky enough to have a lot of responsibility means working hours are long, but after being an athlete getting up at 5.30 a.m. to head to the gym now doesn't feel at all alien. If I don't get my gym session in on the way to work I'm sluggish and grumpy all day so those early starts are definitely worth it! As staff we get the opportunity to take part in Tough Mudder events when we don't have to work at them, so I completed my first one in Yorkshire in 2013.

We hadn't had a wheelchair user do one of the courses in Europe so it was a bit of a trial-and-error undertaking, with ropes and duct tape borrowed from our logistics company and sponsors at the last minute and a team pulled together with a couple of days' notice. It was a pretty epic team though! There aren't many companies where the Managing Director and Operations Director would be happy to pull, push and carry you around 12 miles of mud, through electric-shock wires, over walls, inside tunnels and up a giant quarter pipe. We were joined by four of our most dedicated and impressive Mudders who have run countless laps of our courses since Tough Mudder came to the UK, as well as one of our merchandise partners, all of whom made me feel like I was a useful part of the team rather than the dead weight slowing them down that I'd been worried I would be. I could never have got through even the first mile without them all (as evidenced by the fact I did actually fall out of my chair about 200 m into the run), and what was also really humbling was how everyone who passed us on course would heed my team-mates' shouts to join us and help out for a bit.

That's what makes Tough Mudder so incredible – it's not a race, it's a challenge. As nobody's timed the camaraderie and teamwork you see on course is so different to anything I've seen in a race as there's no incentive to leave team-mates behind to get to the end. It's always the teams who run through the electric wires together at the end, however long they've taken, that get the biggest cheer. Despite how ill I felt for weeks after completing that course (probably due to getting colder than I've even felt in minus-fifty-degree Canadian temperatures!) I can't wait to do it again in 2014 just for that amazing feeling of having achieved something awesome without having had to beat anyone else to get there.

From time to time I tell my friends I'm going to race this race or that race, but in reality I can't see myself getting back on the track anytime soon. Once enough time has passed that I can take part in the London Marathon or Silverstone Half Marathon recreationally without my performance being judged as worse than I used to be, I'd like to give them both another go. For now though I'm happy keeping myself fit and healthy in the gym in winter and outside in summer, and not having to take on the rain and cold or worry if I skip a workout to spend time with friends or family.

Being back in an office has brought home how uncompromising and goal oriented I was as an athlete – and how hard it is to lose those traits. I still have to push as fast as I can even if I'm just in my everyday chair going to the station, and I naturally judge everything I do at work by the numbers and have constant sleepless nights if I haven't hit them, rather than being hugely comfortable with feelings and judgements without data to back them up. I'm learning though, and at times it does feel a bit like a rehabilitation process remembering that not everything has to be achieved right away and in the way I want it to be achieved. Thankfully Tough Mudder is a great place to learn as we are constantly appraised and so I can track where I'm doing well and where I still need to remember to turn the 'human' back on! We also have huge amounts of access to 'Tough Mudder University' learning materials across all subjects in addition to everyone being happy to share their knowledge so I feel like every time I make use of these I become incrementally more able to achieve my future goals.

For over four years after breaking my back I defined myself as an athlete not a disabled person. Readjusting my image of myself after returning to the 'real world' of a full-time office job, complete with hideous London commute, to acknowledge that regardless of whether or not I was racing internationally I was still disabled has been really hard.

What I've realized though, is that as much as I wanted to prove that I could be normal and still climb mountains and do marathons despite being in a wheelchair, it's being in a wheelchair that made me do those things. It sounds a cliché to say that my accident made me determined to live my life to the full but unfortunately it's a cliché that's true – it's been a rollercoaster five years since that day on the Oxford ring road but I hope the next five years are just as eventful. I have some big goals that I want to achieve in my career and in my personal life, but most importantly I hope that in this next half-decade I take more time to stop and take stock of what I've achieved and where I'm falling short as a person, instead of constantly powering on to the next hurdle I want to flatten. Somehow though, I think that's going to be the biggest challenge so far!

Ordinary People, Extraordinary Lives

Share Your Extraordinary Story

Has something amazing happened to you?

Was your life changed forever?

Do you have an incredible story to share?

We want to hear about it, and in your own words. Tell us about you, your life, and what makes it so extraordinary for the chance to have a whole book dedicated to your story and shared with the nation.

Email extraordinary.people@littlebrown.co.uk with a synopsis of your story in 100 words or fewer, plus the first three chapters. Tell us about your life before, how it is now and share as many details as you can. The deadline for applications is midnight on 30 September 2014. Submissions should be a Word document or PDF email attachment.